EMBODIED KNOWLEDGE IN ENSEMBLE PERFORMANCE

SEMPRE Studies in
The Psychology of Music

Series Editors

Graham Welch, *Institute of Education, University of London, UK*
Adam Ockelford, *Roehampton University, UK*
Ian Cross, *University of Cambridge, UK*

The theme for the series is the psychology of music, broadly defined. Topics include: (i) musical development at different ages, (ii) exceptional musical development in the context of special educational needs, (iii) musical cognition and context, (iv) culture, mind and music, (v) micro to macro perspectives on the impact of music on the individual (such as from neurological studies through to social psychology), (vi) the development of advanced performance skills and (vii) affective perspectives on musical learning. The series presents the implications of research findings for a wide readership, including user-groups (music teachers, policy makers, parents), as well as the international academic and research communities. The distinguishing features of the series is this broad focus (drawing on basic and applied research from across the globe) under the umbrella of SEMPRE's distinctive mission, which is to promote and ensure coherent and symbiotic links between education, music and psychology research.

Other titles in the series

Developing the Musician
Contemporary Perspectives on Teaching and Learning
Edited by Mary Stakelum

Music and Familiarity
Listening, Musicology and Performance
Edited by Elaine King and Helen M. Prior

Collaborative Learning in Higher Music Education
Edited by Helena Gaunt and Heidi Westerlund

I Drum, Therefore I Am
Being and Becoming a Drummer
Gareth Dylan Smith

Embodied Knowledge in Ensemble Performance

J. MURPHY McCALEB
Kidderminster College, UK

ASHGATE

Published by
Ashgate Publishing Limited
Wey Court East
Union Road
Farnham
Surrey, GU9 7PT
England

www.ashgate.com

Ashgate Publishing Company
110 Cherry Street
Suite 3-1
Burlington, VT 05401-3818
USA

British Library Cataloguing in Publication Data
A catalogue record for this book is available from the British Library

The Library of Congress has cataloged the printed edition as follows:
McCaleb, J. Murphy.
  Embodied knowledge in ensemble performance / by J. Murphy McCaleb.
    pages ; cm. – (SEMPRE studies in the psychology of music)
  Includes bibliographical references and index.
  ISBN 978-1-4724-1961-3 (hardcover : alk. paper) 1. Ensemble playing. I. Title.
  MT728.M23 2014
  781.4'38–dc23

2013026724

ISBN 9781472419613 (hbk)

Bach musicological font developed by © Yo Tomita

MIX
Paper from
responsible sources
FSC
www.fsc.org   FSC® C013985

Printed in the United Kingdom by Henry Ling Limited, at the Dorset Press, Dorchester, DT1 1HD

For Russ

Contents

List of Figures and Tables   *ix*
List of Music Examples   *xi*
Video Examples   *xiii*
Series Editors' Preface   *xv*
Preface   *xvii*

1   A Question of Ensemble   1

2   Beyond Communication   19

3   A Question of Content   47

4   The Process of Performance   63

5   Reaction and Inter-reaction   83

6   Reflecting on Musical Knowledge   109

Select Bibliography   *127*
Index   *137*

List of Figures and Tables

Figures

1.1   The performance-based cycle of action and reflection   15

Tables

3.1   Examples of metaphor in rehearsal language   51
3.2   The spectrum of musical referents   56

List of Music Examples

2.1   Samuel Barber, *String Quartet No. 1, Op. 11*. Movement II, bars 35–40   43

3.1   Samuel Barber, *String Quartet No. 1, Op. 11*. Movement II, bars 52–53   53

4.1   Samuel Barber, *String Quartet No. 1, Op. 11*. Movement II, bars 35–40   71
4.2   Samuel Barber, *String Quartet No. 1, Op. 11*. Movement II, bars 15–18   72

5.1   Samuel Barber, *String Quartet No. 1, Op. 11*. Movement II, bars 35–40   102
5.2   Samuel Barber, *String Quartet No. 1, Op. 11*. Movement III, bars 39–46   104
5.3   Samuel Barber, *String Quartet No. 1, Op. 11*. Movement I, bars 35–38   106

Video Examples

The attached DVD contains all the video examples referred to within this text. These videos fall into two categories. The first draws from rehearsal footage of the Boult Quartet, taken from 20–23 September, 2010 at Birmingham Conservatoire, UK. I was not present in the room other than to turn the camcorder on and off, instead observing these rehearsals after they had taken place. The members of the Boult Quartet have elected to remain anonymous. The second category of video is from a performance of The Supergroup, taken 17 January 2011, in Birmingham Conservatoire's Recital Hall. The ensemble performed an entirely improvised piece entitled *Waltz of the Tearing Tears*. The members of the ensemble include:

- Seán Clancy, alto saxophone and melodica
- Roberto Alonso Trillo, violin
- Sebastiano Dessanay, double bass
- Tychonas Michailidis, live electronics
- Murphy McCaleb, bass trombone

Video examples from these sources are used throughout this text. Therefore, the examples on the attached DVD are organized relative to their corresponding chapters within this book. Quotations of comments made by musicians on film that do not appear on the DVD are referenced in terms of the rehearsal they took place in, with times in accordance with the raw video footage.

The DVD contents are as follows:

Chapter 2

1. Boult Quartet: Discussion of Samuel Barber, *String Quartet No. 1, Op. 11*. Movement III, bars 41–46
2. Boult Quartet: First rehearsal of Samuel Barber, S*tring Quartet No. 1, Op. 11*. Movement II, bars 35–40
3. Boult Quartet: Second rehearsal of Samuel Barber, *String Quartet No. 1, Op. 11*. Movement II, bars 35–40

Chapter 3

1. Boult Quartet: Discussion of Samuel Barber, *String Quartet No. 1, Op. 11*. Movement II, bars 52–53
2. Boult Quartet: Examples of multimodal exchanges in rehearsal

Chapter 4

1. The Supergroup: Excerpts from *Waltz of the Tearing Tears*
2. Boult Quartet: First rehearsal of Samuel Barber, *String Quartet No. 1, Op. 11*. Movement II, bars 35–40
3. Boult Quartet: Rehearsal of Samuel Barber, *String Quartet No. 1, Op. 11*. Movement II, bars 15–18

Chapter 5

1. Boult Quartet: Second rehearsal of Samuel Barber, S*tring Quartet No. 1, Op. 11*. Movement II, bars 35–40
2. Boult Quartet: Rehearsal of Samuel Barber, *String Quartet No. 1, Op. 11*. Movement III, bars 39–46
3. Boult Quartet: Rehearsal of Samuel Barber, *String Quartet No. 1, Op. 11*. Movement I, bars 35–38

Chapter 6

1. The Supergroup: Excerpts from *Waltz of the Tearing Tears*
2. The Supergroup: Excerpts from *Waltz of the Tearing Tears*

Series Editors' Preface

There has been an enormous growth over the past three decades of research into the psychology of music. SEMPRE (the Society for Education, Music and Psychology Research) is the only international society that embraces an interest in the psychology of music, research and education. SEMPRE was founded in 1972 and has published the journals *Psychology of Music* since 1973 and *Research Studies in Music Education* since 2008, both now in partnership with SAGE (see www.sempre.org.uk). Nevertheless, there is an ongoing need to promote the latest research to the widest possible audience if it is to have a distinctive impact on policy and practice. In collaboration with Ashgate since 2007, the 'SEMPRE Studies in The Psychology of Music' has been designed to address this need. The theme for the series is the psychology of music, broadly defined. Topics include (amongst others): musical development at different ages; musical cognition and context; culture, mind and music; micro to macro perspectives on the impact of music on the individual (such as from neurological studies through to social psychology); the development of advanced performance skills; musical behaviour and development in the context of special educational needs; and affective perspectives on musical learning. The series seeks to present the implications of research findings for a wide readership, including user-groups (music teachers, policy makers, parents), as well as the international academic and research communities. The distinguishing feature of the series is its broad focus that draws on basic and applied research from across the globe under the umbrella of SEMPRE's distinctive mission, which is to promote and ensure coherent and symbiotic links between education, music and psychology research.

Graham Welch
Institute of Education, University of London, UK
Adam Ockelford
Roehampton University, UK
Ian Cross
University of Cambridge, UK

Preface

Chamber music performance can be magic. Those playing share a connectedness and intimacy that surpasses many other social interactions. Individual musicians' interpretations build upon each other to create an aesthetic whole that may be much greater than the sum of its parts. Unexpectedness and spontaneity can spark the most exciting performances, pushing the ensemble members to the boundaries of their technical and creative abilities. It is difficult for any of the musicians to say where the performance will go: the unforeseen creative result may often be the most fulfilling one.

To play chamber music, especially with those skilled in its art, is a joy. I have been lucky enough to spend the majority of my musical career involved in some form of ensemble performance. As a bass trombonist, I have been called upon to play in everything from Renaissance ensembles and brass quintets to funk bands and liturgical groups. The more opportunities I have to perform with such ensembles, the more I realize that it is not just the music that enchants me. Participation in small ensemble performance is exciting because of the level of interaction it requires. While pursuing a postgraduate degree in chamber music at the University of Michigan, I became increasingly aware of the intricacies inherent in ensemble interaction. My love for small ensemble performance and my efforts to become the best chamber musician I could be provided the impetus behind my doctoral programme of study.

The initial intent for this research was to classify both the gestures being used and the social roles that may be exhibited within ensemble performance. I attempted to make musical practice fit within existing theories of social interaction, interpreting it as if it were purely a psychological or sociological phenomenon. As my work progressed, discrepancies arose between what I was reading and my experiences as a musician. Superficially, it appeared that the application of psychological and sociological theories was a fruitful approach to explaining ensemble interaction. However, I increasingly found fundamental questions remained unanswered. Musical experience itself became the best tool for practical research. Applied research from other fields, I realized, was a means to an end, not an end in itself. This allowed me to focus my attention on identifying the processes inherent within ensemble performance. Out of my musical practice, new theoretical propositions could be formed, resulting in the book as it stands today.

As will be discussed throughout this text, the impact of practical musical knowledge should not be underestimated within musicological performance studies. The application of this knowledge to existing theories of performance provides an invaluable critical tool by which these theories may be tested. In a similar fashion, academic research into performance may inform musicians' understanding of how ensembles function, encouraging the development of new pedagogical methods. It is from this perspective that this book is written: not only to expand upon the propositional knowledge generated from academic research into musical performance, but to provide theoretical underpinnings to the procedural knowledge used every day by performers. By extension, the conclusions arrived at through the application of nonmusical academic fields may yield positive results when applied to the concerns of those fields.

I have only been able to write this book through the continued support and assistance from a large network of colleagues, friends and family. Whilst I cannot name them all without adding an additional chapter, I would like to recognize a few of those people so important to me. Rest assured, absence of someone's name does not mean they are absent from my thoughts.

My doctoral advisory panel was exemplary throughout my degree. In particular, Professor Peter Johnson has been instrumental in encouraging me to turn a critical and imaginative eye to my practice, my research and my beliefs. My time with him has shown me that researching music does not take away its magic: increased understanding only emphasizes its status as an object of fascination and wonder. Conversations with Professor John Sparrow instigated a dramatic shift in perspective towards the beginning of my degree, reminding me of the wealth of knowledge that can be found within practice itself. Ensuring that I do not abuse 'the Queen's English', Dr Carrie Churnside never turned down a request to proofread my work, even when she was on sabbatical. In addition, Dr Liz Garnett provided valuable critique in my preparation of multiple conference papers.

I could not have conducted this research without being at an institution that was willing to let me observe and participate in as many musical ensembles as I could physically attend. The faculty and students at Birmingham Conservatoire enthusiastically cooperated with me throughout my degree, creating a warm, welcoming environment. After being forewarned that my doctorate would be one of the loneliest times of my life, I was pleasantly surprised to find that the opposite was true. I would like to thank two particular ensembles for their extensive collaboration. First, the Boult Quartet, the senior student quartet at Birmingham Conservatoire during my first two years, graciously allowed themselves to be video-recorded by me on multiple occasions. The arguments presented throughout this book would not be possible if not for the excerpts from their rehearsals permeating the text. Second, my doctoral colleagues in The Supergroup – Seán Clancy, Roberto Alonso Trillo, Sebastiano Dessanay and Tychonas Michailidis – provided critique and inspiration to the topics discussed throughout this book. Along with Joanna Szalewska-Pineau and Carolina Noguera-Palau, they were integral to my doctoral experience. I wish them all the best in the completion of their degrees and their assuredly successful careers. Finally, I cannot help but thank Liz Reeve, the administrative lynchpin that holds the Conservatoire's research department together.

With respect to my life inside and outside of my doctorate, I would like to thank my parents, Barbara and David McCaleb. Even after I decided to move halfway around the world, they continually support me in every endeavour, including combing through this book in search of typos. Clare Bailey has been by my side day in and day out, even while she became a doctor as well. I would not be on the career path I am on now if it were not for Dr Karen Fournier and Dr James Bicigo, who recognized my interests and aptitude before even I had thought about pursuing a doctorate. I am grateful for their constant encouragement and insight. Last (but certainly not least), I would like to thank Dr Laura Walters for not only her proofreading skills, but also her immeasurable advice on successfully conducting a doctorate while living 4000 miles from home.

JMM
January 2014

Chapter 1
A Question of Ensemble

As the rehearsal begins, the members of my low brass trio go about their individual business of preparation. I blow air and a few random notes through my bass trombone, the French horn player oils a particularly aggravating valve and the tenor trombonist pulls her case alongside her chair so as to have a metronome and tuner at hand. Upon deciding which piece we will work on, a transcription of a trio sonata by Arcangelo Corelli, we further determine the movement to play. We agree to run through it first, to give us an idea of the overall state of readiness of the movement for performance. After tuning, we settle into our performing positions: the horn player and I put our instruments to our lips and make eye contact while the tenor trombonist sits up and keeps an eye on her part. With a quiet, steady breath, we begin to play. My part, the lowest, creates a moving line against that of the more sedate horn. I bob slightly with the larger pulse and try to give a sense of line that matches the longer phrases in the other part. The trombonist joins us, her preparatory breath feeling more like a continuation of previous events than the first notes of her part. Against the lingering notes above me, I constantly try to gauge my tuning, matching up every interval so that none draw attention to themselves. Gradually, the upper two musicians expand their tone qualities, their original *piano* blossoming into a weightier sound. Just as they try to stay consistent harmonically, I focus on solid timekeeping, my moving line underpinning the other parts. Dissonances become a joy, and we begin to make the most of their resolutions. I can tell that the hornist and the trombonist, whose parts balance between unison, dissonance and resolution, are constantly adjusting their intonation to the sounds around them. Occasionally, we land on a chord that resonates not only our instruments, but our bodies as well – one of the great pleasures of acoustic performance. We near the end of the short movement, feeling the momentum of the piece decrease. Easing into the last few chords, my physical bobbing increases slightly as my quavers lengthen. Arriving at the final chord, we relax and feel the movement dissipate into the space around us. We end with an almost imperceptible nod, keeping our instruments up for a moment until it feels as if the piece has properly finished.

This narrative, drawn from a typical rehearsal, highlights processes that continually take place within ensemble performance. In this context, musical performance does not require a non-performing audience, simply the communal production of music. The example chosen to start this book might have come from any number of rehearsals or performances by any number of ensembles and illustrates the types of thoughts, concerns and experiences of an ensemble musician in the Western classical tradition. As a bass trombonist who has focused on chamber music performance, my understanding of what it means to create music with other people is filled with such memories and experiences. Playing music together is not a single activity, but encompasses a spectrum of processes, ranging from the more quantifiable rhythmic synchronization and adjustment of intonation to the more elusive coordination of dynamics, phrasing and interpretation. These processes are all necessary for the creation of a cohesive musical performance and are unique to performing music within an ensemble.

This book explores musical interaction as found in small ensemble performance. Although the conclusions reached through the discussions found in this text may be valid for non-Western musical traditions, complexities easily arise from attempts to generalize across multiple cultures and musical heritages. Whilst I will make efforts to point out similarities between the conclusions of my research and existing ethnomusicological literature, I must stress that my formal performance background and research specialities are in Western classical music and jazz. Therefore, throughout this book I will primarily discuss ensemble interaction within Western art music.

Although musicians have played in ensembles as long as musical performance has been in existence and, to this day, can still teach successive musicians best practice when involved in ensembles, theoretical knowledge of the procedural underpinnings of small ensemble interaction is incomplete. Recent academic research on ensemble interaction approaches the topic from a primarily sociological stance. This work is beneficial in that it allows researchers to frame this topic within established concepts of interpersonal dynamics. That said, the uniqueness of musical groups among other collections of people is recognized by psychologists Vivienne Young and Andrew Colman, who describe ensembles as 'an unusual kind of social group whose mode of interaction involves a degree of intimacy and subtlety possibly not equalled by any other kind of group' (1979: 12). Given the idiosyncratic nature of the interaction that takes place in musical ensembles, previous research on group performance may be considered to be the pursuit of a framework or paradigm from another field that can be applied best within a musical context. This search has provided a host of possibilities drawn from the fields of psychology,[1] sociology,[2] conversation studies and linguistics,[3] neurology and cognitive studies,[4] and even ergonomics.[5] However, as will be seen, this body of literature is inadequate as the primary means of understanding musical ensembles, particularly because insufficient attention is

---

[1]   Blank and Davidson, 2007; Garnett, 2009; and Ginsborg et al., 2006.

[2]   Davidson, 1997; Davidson and Good, 2002; Ford and Davidson, 2003; King, 2006a, 2006b; King and Ginsborg, 2011; Murnighan and Conlon, 1991; Seddon and Biasutti, 2009; and Young and Colman, 1979.

[3]   Davidson, 2005; Davidson and King, 2004; Sawyer, 2005; and Williamon and Davidson, 2002.

[4]   Garnett, 2009; Manduell and Wing, 2007; and Tovstiga et al., 2004.

[5]   Davidson, 2005.

given to the practical knowledge performers have acquired through experience within ensembles themselves.

Regardless of its apparent suitability, the wealth of interdisciplinary sources upon which this research is drawn is primarily concerned with verbal interaction between group members. Research on the balance of activities during rehearsal has noted that chamber groups tend to spend the majority of their rehearsal time playing rather than engaging in verbal discussion.[6] The mechanisms for determining musical variables such as tempo, dynamics, intonation, phrasing and interpretation must therefore emerge during this form of social musicking. Whilst these mechanisms exist within a single musician during solo performance, ensemble performance necessitates the simultaneous consideration of these variables between multiple individuals. The emphasis that musicians give to nonverbal interaction suggests that research into ensemble interaction should accordingly focus on the communal act of making music. Therefore, I may pose the first of four research questions below.

1. How do musicians interact and share information with each other while performing?

In order to comprehensively address this question, it is necessary to identify and highlight what actually happens during ensemble musical performance. Needless to say, the primary activity occurring during instrumental performance is the operation of a musical instrument.[7] Albeit straightforward, this fundamental element has previously only been the focus of pedagogical materials specific to each instrument or family of instruments. That being said, recent research on performance has begun to investigate the cognitive frameworks underlying musicians' actions with the intent of quantifying and categorizing physical gestures used during performance (Davidson, 2012; Godøy and Leman, 2010). From a practical perspective, however, it may be more important to identify how musical content may affect the ways that performers have to interact with their instruments instead of creating a gestural typology. A firm grasp of the relationships between musical content and the actions required in playing it is necessary to understand the practical processes integrated within ensemble performance.

This first research question makes the assumption that we know the nature and characteristics of the information being shared amongst performers. This may not be the case. Whilst one could simply say that such information pertains to the variables of the music being played, such an answer may be too general. Is the information being shared purely of a musical nature (that is to say, relating to variables such as tempo, dynamic, intonation, phrasing and interpretation) or does it involve other 'extramusical' elements? May this information exist in other

---

[6] Blank and Davidson, 2007; Blum, 1987; Seddon and Biasutti, 2009; Tovstiga et al., 2004; and Williamon and Davidson, 2002.

[7] In vocal performance, the voice naturally serves as a musical instrument, as it has its own idiosyncratic operation distinct from that of speech.

forms or be expressed through different media? I would argue that it is impossible to fully understand the medium by which information is transferred without understanding (at least partially) the qualities of the information itself. Thus, in order to comprehensively answer the first research question, it is necessary to solidify understanding of the information being shared.

2. WHAT IS THE NATURE OF THE INFORMATION BEING SHARED IN ENSEMBLE PERFORMANCE?
Regardless of the theoretical issues that surround the nature of 'musical information' (should such information be deemed purely musical), such information may correlate to a certain degree with the specific musical content that is being performed. If so, how may this correlation be reflected in the individual performances of each musician? It is therefore necessary to consider the phenomenological experience of individual musicians.

3. TO WHAT EXTENT DOES THE MUSICAL CONTENT BEING PERFORMED AFFECT THE WAYS IT HAS TO BE PHYSICALLY CREATED BY MUSICIANS?
Consequently, the fourth research question combines elements of the first three.

4. HOW DOES THE PHYSICAL RELATIONSHIP BETWEEN THE PERFORMER AND THEIR INSTRUMENT RELATE TO COMMUNICATIVE AND INTERACTIVE PROCESSES OF ENSEMBLE PERFORMANCE?
By isolating the ways that individual musicians act during performance, this book investigates ensemble interaction as found in musical performance itself, rather than within verbal discussion. Therefore, it provides the basis upon which ensemble performance may be understood in a way not dependent upon the limited paradigm of verbal communication. As these research questions are contingent upon an examination of the intimate relationship between a musician and their instrument, the tacit understanding that musicians have of this interconnection must be acknowledged. Revealing propositional knowledge from within embedded procedural knowledge is further problematized by the methodological issues pertaining to capturing and comprehending human experience. This book addresses these concerns through the applied use of reflective practice, as described later in this chapter.

The research questions detailed above provide a framework for this book. Rather than structuring the book in a manner that lays out background material, hypothesis, methodology, results and discussion in a strict order, I have chosen to present my work more organically. This allows me to lead the reader through the same development of argument and thought processes that occurred within my own research. Likewise, this format provides easier reference to some of the interdisciplinary fields that are drawn upon throughout my argument, rather than simply providing a large amount of seemingly disparate background information through a literature review. Chapter 2 examines modes of communication within ensemble interaction as well as how leadership may function in this specialized social context. Through this discussion, previous sociological models that have been applied to musicological research are critiqued in addition to more fundamental concepts such as inter-performer communication in music. Chapter 3 explores the nature and kinds of information that may be shared amongst ensemble performers. By examining rehearsal language, this chapter raises questions about phenomenology of musical experience, both as a performer and listener. Progressing to the third research question, Chapter 4 focuses upon the ways in which musicians interact with their instruments, particularly considering how these interactions may be affected by individual performers' musical intentions. This discussion requires an examination of the phenomenology of solo instrumental performance and critique of previous cognitive models. Increasingly, my research will stress that performance requires unique forms of knowledge intrinsically tied to the experience of making music. From this perspective, Chapter 5 considers the experience of the performer from within an ensemble. Drawing upon the conclusions found in the previous chapters, I examine how musicians' individual performances may exert influences on that of their fellow ensemble members. After addressing the four primary research questions, further threads of discussion will be examined in the sixth and final chapter. In particular, I will demonstrate the ways in which the proposals found throughout this book may inform the wider sphere of research on performative musical knowledge. Similarly, the final chapter will include speculation upon the applicability of the musicological research I have conducted on the non-musicological fields that have been drawn upon throughout the book.

This introductory chapter begins with an overview of the literature and associated academic fields that are currently at play in ensemble research of Western art music. It must be noted that this is not the place for an exhaustive review of background literature; in-depth assessment of this literature will be presented where pertinent throughout the text. Following this overview is a critique of the methods drawn upon in previous research on ensemble interaction. In light of the research questions posed at the beginning of this chapter, it is necessary to re-examine the kind of knowledge under consideration when engaging in performance studies. After clarifying the ways in which contrasting forms of knowledge will be examined within this book, an alternative methodological approach is presented that may more suitably address both my research questions and any additional epistemological concerns. I will return to this methodological approach in Chapter 6 in a critique of its efficacy and applicability to research on musical performance.

Investigating Ensemble Performance

The research questions posed in this book are designed to investigate the mechanisms of ensemble interaction in a way that benefits both active musicians and researchers. Due to this approach, these investigations often blur boundaries between academic disciplines, moving from sociology to philosophy to music theory to neurology within the same discussion. The following section outlines the fields and concepts drawn upon throughout this text so as to clarify the intellectual terrain to be explored. From this standpoint, it will be possible to critique the most common methodologies used within ensemble research and other related fields. This will lay the groundwork necessary to describe and rationalize the methodological approach used within this book.

Current musicological literature on ensemble interaction categorizes ensemble interaction in relation to verbal and nonverbal modes of communication, most notably described by Frederick Seddon (2005). With regard to nonverbal communication (the focus of this book), Alexander Jensenius et al. have identified four categories of gestures that may be made during performance: sound-producing, sound-facilitating, sound-accompanying and communicative (2010: 23). Communicative gestures have historically been the primary focus of research on gesture in performance and are interpreted primarily through two models. The first approach, reliant upon a linguistic model of communication, prioritizes the identification and categorization of physical gestures in a semantic manner.[8] Therefore, conclusions regarding performers' gestures have arisen in part from research into gestures used during speech,[9] and have been primarily orientated toward communicative signalling between the performer and the audience (Davidson, 2005; Windsor, 2011). The second approach avoids linguistic parallels, proposing that musicians' gestures in performance are not grounded in semantics but instead are indications of interior mental states (Elsdon, 2006). Both of these theoretical models of communication are the result of observation of video-recorded performances. As will become evident, this body of research rarely examines the effects performers' gestures may have on their fellow musician, and when it does, it presumes a similar relationship as that between performer and audience. However, the interaction between ensemble musicians fundamentally differs from that between performer and audience in that coperformers need to coordinate and execute technical actions in order to perform effectively. Coordination of these actions requires some form of implicit or explicit transfer of information (Tovstiga et al., 2004: 9).

Adequate consideration of the first research question requires more than simply an appraisal of the physical gestures that may be used in performance. In addition, it is necessary to examine how leadership may operate within ensembles. This area of research has exclusively approached the question of musical leadership through applied sociological models such as those developed by business theorist James Burns (1978). Recalling that ensembles interact both verbally and nonverbally, it is useful to differentiate this body of literature in terms of these categories. Research on verbally articulated leadership presupposes that musical leadership operates outside performance, considering ensembles as a variant of other goal-oriented groups.[10] Contrary to this approach is research on leadership through physical gesture, which addresses how leadership may be

---

[8]   Clarke and Davidson, 1998; Davidson, 2001, 2005.
[9]   Ekman and Friesen, 1969; McNeill and Duncan, 2000.
[10] Young and Colman, 1979; Murnighan and Conlon, 1991.

exhibited within performance itself.[11] Whilst these two theoretical models are concerned with the expression of leadership within different contexts, both focus on identifying leadership patterns among ensemble members, ascribing traditional (non-music specific) group roles to musicians. Given this inherent sociological predisposition, it follows that this research is dependent upon observation, interviews and surveys of practitioner literature.

The second research question calls for an investigation into the characteristics of the information being shared in an ensemble. Through the overview of literature found in Chapter 2, however, it will become apparent that current ensemble research fails to address concerns both over the content being communicated between performers and the appropriateness of a communicative paradigm as the basis for understanding ensemble interaction. An examination and application of Lakoff and Johnson's concept of metaphor provides the foundation upon which the relationship of music to the human mind may be understood (1980). Whilst this research has found parallels in musical analysis,[12] there has yet to be extensive investigation on the use of metaphor in understanding performance. Similarly, research on ensemble interaction has extensively focused on the paradigm of communication, drawing upon its process of encoding, transmitting and decoding information and its associated linguistic terms. With continued references to 'nonverbal communication' (King and Ginsborg, 2011), 'communicative gestures' (Dahl et al., 2010), 'modes of communication' (Seddon and Biasutti, 2009) and 'visual communication' (Kokotsaki, 2007) among others, this body of research maintains the tacit assumption that musical performers operate in a manner similar to those involved in conversation. However, this paradigm encourages a framework of understanding that is rooted not in musical performance but in social interaction. The use of a communicative paradigm for ensemble interaction is critiqued in Chapter 2, allowing for the establishment of a new paradigm based on performance itself.

An exploration of the direct physical relationship between musician and instrument, the third research question, prompts an investigation into how humans create and experience musical phenomena through performance. Whilst the term 'phenomena' may be defined primarily as the object of one's perception, for the purposes of this book I use it to refer to a musical act involving both intention and realization. When considering how individuals interact within performance, it is important to distinguish between one's personal intentions and the intentions as perceived by observers; consequently, the concept of attributed intention will be considered later in the book in relation to the fourth research question. There has been little research on the phenomenon of individual performance to date other than neurological studies on how music engages with the human brain (Altenmüller et al., 2006). Whilst this book will call upon some neurological

---

[11] Goodman, 2002; Davidson and King, 2004; King and Ginsborg, 2011; Manduell and Wing, 2007; Williamon and Davidson, 2002.

[12] Saslaw, 1996; Zbikowski, 2008, 2009.

research, it will not be the primary focus. Rather, discussion will be driven by an understanding of performance from the perspective and experience of a performing musician. This is not to say that neurological studies do not have an impact upon musicological research; however, from the frame of reference of an active musician, such medical research has not thus far been expressed in such a way as to affect the practice of performance.[13] Therefore, this book will investigate the aspects of sensory experience engaged during musical performance that can be identified by the performer themselves. Current research in this area emerges from the application of case studies and experiments conducted by cognitive theorists and experimental philosophers.[14] After establishing the general processes by which musicians can create sound on their instruments, it is then necessary to consider how that fundamental ability may develop into skilled, fluent musical performance. An understanding of this development requires both a review of the acquisition of skill in musical performance as well as consideration of current pedagogical literature.[15]

The potential effects the relationship between musician and instrument can have on the social dynamics of ensemble performance, the fourth research question, has not been explicitly researched to date. As early as the late 1970s, temporal synchronization was extensively explored through the analysis of sound recordings and their corresponding spectrograms (Rasch, 1979). However, coordination of other musical variables such as dynamics, expression and interpretation have remained peripheral to this area of study. Through the first three research questions, it will be possible to discuss interpretative coordination in a manner directly rooted in performance. Although such coordination has been briefly mentioned by Goodman (2002) and Williamon and Davidson (2002), the sorts of information that are shared between performers and the process of knowledge transfer has not yet been identified. Given the balance of research conducted thus far, less attention will be paid to temporal synchronization than to the shared understanding of other musical variables. Likewise, from my perspective as a performer, the admittedly important act of coordinating tempi among my fellow musicians does not have as large an impact on the resulting performance as the collaboration of interpretation. An understanding of interpretative coordination should encourage clarification of the processes inherent in the temporal synchronization, whereas the opposite may not necessarily be true.

The final step in understanding ensemble interaction is to consider how the phenomenon of individual performance may be altered within an ensemble context. Primarily, this requires exploration of how inference may function within musical

---

[13]   In other words, whilst it may be objectively interesting to understand what part of the brain is activated during performance, there has yet to be an effective way to relate this information to practical musical activities.

[14]   Elsner and Hommel, 2001; Hoffmann et al., 2004; and Tomasello et al., 2005.

[15]   Barry and Hallam, 2002; Keller and Koch, 2008; Pecenka and Keller, 2009; and Halmrast et al., 2010.

performance. In this manner, the previous discussion on intention may be extended to focus on how musical intention may be attributed to fellow performers. In addition, psychological research on humans' ability to deduce information through visual observation (conducted through the use of laboratory experiments) provides the background necessary to comprehend advanced inferential processes.[16] From this perspective, research on the continuous adaptation that occurs in improvised ensembles may be applied to chamber groups.[17] This research, rooted in performance observation and interviews with skilled musicians, highlights some of the general processes that may occur within musical interaction.

Methodological Considerations

In order to effectively explore the research questions posed at the beginning of this chapter, it is necessary to consider the methods used within the aforementioned research. Through such a critique, it is possible to arrive at a methodological approach that will suitably address the theoretical, practical and epistemological issues that emerge from ensemble research.

A favourite theoretical approach amongst musicologists researching ensemble performance has been to consider physical gesture as a form of communication. Given this tacit assumption, empirical musicological research has utilized a variety of methodologies, each emphasizing a slightly different aspect of communication. Many of these methodologies borrow heavily from those developed in the social sciences, particularly observation, interviews and surveys, analysis of practitioner literature, and laboratory experiments. Application of these methods to musicological research has illustrated, to varying degrees, the significant differences between musical ensembles and other social groups. The following assessment of these methods reveals their potential benefits to this field as well as highlighting aspects of musical performance that evade traditional sociological inquiry. From this critique emerges issues surrounding how best to investigate the kind of knowledge involved in skilled practice. It is only through a firm grasp of this form of knowledge that an appropriate and effective methodological framework may be created.

One of the primary methods used in sociological research on ensembles is observation. This allows for the documentation of the actions of ensemble members and, in the case of video recording, a prolonged period for their analysis and review. That being said, there are three particular limits to the knowledge gained through observation. First, by its nature, this method clearly delineates between those under scrutiny and those conducting research. Whilst an observer may see and hear an ensemble in operation, there is no way for them to fully experience what is going on from within the ensemble at that given time: they are

---

[16] Runeson and Frykholm, 1981 and 1983.

[17] Tovstiga et al., 2004; Sawyer, 2005; and Kokotsaki, 2007.

outside of the ensemble, looking in. Second, the conclusions arrived at through observation cannot be easily generalized or directly applied to other specific cases. Individuals' personal and mechanical idiosyncrasies are not necessarily indicative of common human attributes – a point emphasized by Mario Wiesendanger et al. in their research on motor control in violin performance (2006: 112). Third, the interactions between coperformers can often be too subtle or quick to be noticed through casual observation. Motion capture may assuage this issue through the identification of every movement taking place in performance, although the ability to detect movements in performance is secondary to understanding their meaning or gauging their significance.

Unlike observation, interviews and surveys allow researchers to analyse the interactions of ensembles through the experiences of the participating musicians. The personalized accounts exposed through interviews may provide insight into the unique processes that occur in ensembles. Surveys yield information from larger pools of practitioners, increasing the credibility of any generalizations arising from such research. However, whilst they draw directly upon the knowledge of performers themselves, both interviews and surveys have two limitations: timescale and critical rigour. Due to the amount of time necessary for participant response (especially in the case of surveys), these methods are often conducted in situations so far removed from rehearsal and performance that they are forced to gloss over important details. The rehearsal narrative given at the beginning of this chapter provides an example of this problem; although I can generalize attributes from many rehearsals into a single cohesive representation, I cannot remember the entirety of my experience from a single event, especially in a level of detail necessary for academic research. Likewise, the questions used within surveys often need to be broad enough to elicit responses from a variety of participants. Whilst a large response rate is desirable, it may be at the expense of engaging with precise aspects of performance. Without completely discounting the information gained from interviews and surveys, a lack of specificity reduces their practical applicability and critical rigour.

Practitioner literature, in the same vein as interviews and surveys, allows access to perspectives that are normally restricted to those embedded within musical practice. In addition, the topics under discussion are specifically chosen by the performers themselves. Whilst insightful, this literature has historically been oriented toward a popular (rather than academic) readership, usually detailing the social elements involved in being a professional musician. This is not to say that a lack of scientific rigour discounts the usefulness of this resource. In her work on choral conducting, Liz Garnett suggests that 'the anecdotal assertions from the practitioner literature … arguably present a greater theoretical robustness than the empirical studies that critique them, in that they represent conclusions drawn from a range of experiences, even if that process of abstraction is unsystematic and/ or under-documented' (2009: 28). It is worth considering the broad applicability of this literature, although particular areas may have to be re-examined in a more

critical manner. Likewise, practitioner literature may provide a foil against which to measure the conclusions that emerge from academic research.

Whereas surveys and practitioner literature may provide general information on ensemble interaction, specific aspects of this phenomenon have been closely examined through laboratory experiments and case studies. By isolating variables and limiting the fields of inquiry to restricted situations, controlled studies can provide the scientific rigour to support general theories presented by practitioners. Advances in computer technology such as the increased accessibility of motion capture allow for heightened precision and technical analysis of the ways that performers operate, both alone and within ensemble settings. However, with these benefits come two main drawbacks to clinical research. First, experiments and case studies may lack the spontaneity and authenticity of uninhibited musical interaction. The construction of an artificial context may not adequately reveal how ensembles interact on a daily basis. Second, the sheer amount of data produced does not necessarily presuppose the development of applicable conclusions. Whilst experiments and case studies are useful tools, critical reception of the data is necessary in order to both relate conclusions to practitioners' experiences and to situate them in terms of larger theories.

Modes of Knowledge

Permeating the lineages of research and the associated methods described above is an issue that complicates interdisciplinary research within performance studies. Skilled musical performance relies on a fundamentally different form of knowledge from that which is created through academic research. The knowledge generated by researchers and that by practitioners are categorized by management theorist John Heron as Mode 1 and Mode 2 knowledge, building upon Gilbert Ryle's distinction between propositional and procedural knowledge (Heron, 1999 citing Ryle, 1949). Difficulties arise when attempts are made to transition between these two modes. Not only are they articulated in different manners – Mode 1 through language, Mode 2 through action – but they are created by and for different entities. In the case of performance studies, the two modes of knowledge correlate to the two parties involved in empirical musicological research; academic musicologists generally create and deal with Mode 1 knowledge whilst practitioners create and deal with Mode 2 knowledge. In addition to creating separate forms of knowledge, both groups have unique methods of knowledge retention and dissemination. Empirical researchers assemble their findings into prose, allowing for literary dissemination to other academics. Whilst some performers disseminate their knowledge through written means (particularly in the case of pedagogical writings), most knowledge is passed on through performance itself.

Historically, there has been resistance to considering such skilled activities as being expressions of knowledge. As Roland Barthes commented in the 1970s, 'we are still, and more than ever, a civilization of writing, writing and speech continuing to be the full terms of the informational structure' (1977: 38). Through the latter half of the twentieth century, however, there has been an increasing recognition of the value of non-linguistic knowledge structures within academia. Although the distinction between Mode 1 and Mode 2 knowledge has become accepted in sociological fields, particularly occupational psychology, recognition of these two modes of knowledge has yet to gain significant traction within musicological research on performance. Throughout this book, I examine ways in which this bipartite conception of knowledge may inform theoretical and practical understanding of musical performance.

Due to the division between those groups which deal exclusively with Mode 1 or Mode 2 knowledge, their relationship is often described in terms of insiders and outsiders: emic and etic, in anthropological terms (Harris, 1976: 330). Insiders are those within the system being studied, actively creating Mode 2 knowledge as a by-product of their activities. Outsiders are those who are external to those being studied, either physically, socially or culturally, engaging more directly with Mode 1 knowledge. The combination of the differing forms of knowledge created and contrary physical, social or cultural positioning can result in isolating the two groups from each other. In order for research on musical performance to be useful and applicable to both the academic and practising communities, it is vital that such research avoids (or, at the very least, acknowledges) the possible insider/ outsider dichotomy.

Reflecting on methods currently used in ensemble research, methodologies that utilize interviews, surveys and practitioner literature draw upon Mode 2 knowledge in ways that minimize the tension normally felt between insiders and outsiders. As we have seen, however, none of these methods can easily provide conclusions that are usefully applicable to both groups. In his research on gestural studies in performance, Marc Leman proposes a pluralistic approach to methodology that, whilst motivated by the complexity of gestural studies, may allow for integration of these two modes of knowledge. He writes that:

> the study of gestures cannot be reduced to merely objective measurements of sounds and body movements, nor to simply descriptions of personal experiences and interpretations thereof … The concept of gesture is too complex to be understood from one single methodological perspective, even when considered purely from the viewpoint of an empirical approach. (2010: 149)

This suggests that a combination of approaches would be most effective, drawing on both informed observation and critical, 'real world' practice. The following section explores what an amalgamated methodological approach to ensemble research might entail, providing background and rationale for the methods used within this research.

Considering Action Research

In order to build upon the strengths of the methods described above, a unifying framework is necessary to tie together and effectively orientate research.[18] Otherwise, any attempt at a holistic approach to ensemble research will succumb to fragmentation or an overabundance of raw data. I propose that action research, a methodology developed through the fields of occupational psychology and sociology, could provide a structure within which to utilize the standard methods of empirical musicological research. The rationale for drawing upon this methodology can be found not only in the organization of action research, but also in its underlying philosophical ideas.

Action research is a sociological methodology that allows the people being studied to become part of the knowledge creation process. Mary Brydon-Miller explains that the methodology goes 'beyond the notion that theory can inform practice, to a recognition that theory can and should be generated through practice' (2003: 15). This ideology often has ethical implications in that it allows the possibility of both socially responsible and socially oriented problem solving (Ibid.: 13). Rather than conducting research for the sake of pure academic inquiry, the underlying tenets of action research reveal cooperative intention on the part of the researchers and practitioners, both in terms of the work conducted and the results concluded.

From a structural standpoint, action research can be described as a cycle of action and reflection. Within this framework is enough flexibility to allow specific variations to be developed in order to meet contextual requirements. This adaptability has enabled action research to be applied to a variety of fields, including organization development, anthropology, education, economics, psychology, sociology and management (Ibid.: 12). Stephen Kemmis provides a standard layout of an action research methodology, tailoring it towards a sociological or management-based study. He divides the cycle of action and reflection into four stages:

1. To develop a *plan* of action to improve what is already happening.
2. To *act* to implement the plan.
3. To *observe* the effects of action in the context in which it occurs.
4. To *reflect* on these effects as a basis for further planning, subsequent action and so on, through a succession of cycles.

(1982: 7; my emphasis)

Within this framework, there is a constant, parallel evolution of both action and critical examination. This system is often therefore described not simply as a cycle but as a spiral – the repetition of similar processes on continuously evolving material.

---

[18] Material from this discussion developed from a presentation I gave at the Royal Musical Association Study Day: Collaborations in Practice Led Research at the University of Leeds (October 2010).

Action research is accordingly flexible in the kind of personnel needed to conduct it. Whilst there are many variations, each with their own balance between insiders and outsiders, two appear to be particularly applicable to musicological research: participatory action research and reflective practice. Participatory action research combines the specialized theoretical knowledge of academic researchers with the applied expertise of practitioners through direct interaction with each other (Herr and Anderson, 2005: 9). This approach enables both groups to draw on their specific forms of knowledge and resources to address a single issue. The overarching emphasis on cooperation has made this form of action research favoured in social and economic development projects as well as research on education. The success of this method relies on a moderated balance of input between the two participants; otherwise, it may transform into either standard empirical research or an entirely non-rigorous endeavour.

Reflective practice, on the other hand, encourages practitioners to develop the ability to critically examine their own actions (Schön, 1983). By doing so, they can not only become better at their craft but also document the process by which they expand their specific field of knowledge. This method requires practitioners to take it upon themselves to practise critical inquiry in a well-documented and rigorous manner. In his book *The Reflective Practitioner* (1983), Donald Schön examines instances of reflective practice in action, presenting examples of occupations in which it works (architecture, psychoanalysis) and does not work (city planning). Even in professions most suited to reflective practice, however, the primary obstacle to development in the field is that of dissemination: 'because of the differences in feel for media, language, and repertoire, the art of one practice tends to be opaque to the practitioners of another' (Ibid.: 271). Thus, conclusions drawn from reflective practice need to be demonstrated or clarified in mediums accessible to others. Furthermore, in order for insights to be shared in other fields, they need to be explained in such a way as to enter the parlance of general academia (at the very minimum). Otherwise, any advances would not be understandable or applicable to anyone outside a specific field.

The issues surrounding the dissemination and applicability of Mode 2 knowledge to other fields can be identified as one of the strongest motivating factors for using action research. Kathryn Herr and Gary Anderson remark that 'we cannot escape the basic problems of knowledge generation by elevating practitioners' accounts of practice to a privileged status. That is why collaborative and participatory forms of research among insiders and outsiders hold so much promise' (2005: 53). Using practitioner literature is not enough; there needs to be an understanding of the implications of that literature (comprehension from the practitioner's point of view) in order to make full use of this resource. Overcoming issues of perspective and enculturated knowledge is of primary concern when considering the use of action research methodologies within musicological performance studies, and will be addressed further in this book.

I propose that the spiral of practice and reflection found within action research could serve both to acknowledge and utilize the insider/outsider dichotomy in empirical musicological research. Rather than conducting research *on* musicians and the way they interact with each other, a methodology that combines participatory action research, reflective practice and empirical methods would allow for research *by* and *with* musicians. As Hilary Huang explains, 'action research … always includes practitioners as partners in the work of knowledge creation' (2010: 95). The knowledge created through this research should therefore be applicable to both practising musicians and academic researchers: accessible and useful through both Mode 1 and Mode 2 formats. Acknowledging the merits and epistemological issues surrounding empirical methods such as observation, interviews, literature review and case studies when applied to ensemble research, I aim to maximize their benefits through their utilization within an action research framework.

This pluralistic methodology, reliant upon the practitioners involved, is tailored specifically for research on ensemble interaction. In this model, the locus of critical reflection shifts subtly back and forth between performer and researcher (if they are two separate entities) as the spiral progresses. The actions of both sides are designed to directly influence the other in a symbiotic relationship (see Figure 1.1 for a diagram of this model).

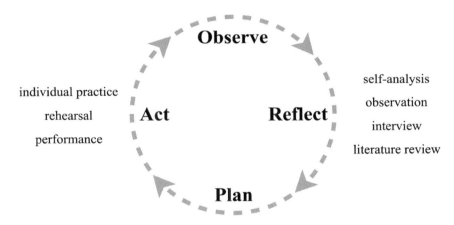

Figure 1.1   The performance-based cycle of action and reflection

In this model, the performer acts as a reflective practitioner in their normal musical activities. Their behaviour motivates the action side of the spiral, encompassing the planning and acting stages. Both musician and researcher initially plan which aspect of musical interaction will be under consideration. This allows for any necessary preparation to find an optimal environment in which to conduct the research: not necessarily to create an artificial situation, but to identify what 'naturally occurring' musical situation might allow for ideal examination of the subject under inquiry. From there, the musician acts and simultaneously observes, participating in their ensemble as they would normally. To a degree, this requires them to temporarily 'forget' that they are acting as a researcher and allow their musical training and experience to motivate their actions. Cognitive distance from a performance as it is happening may discourage (or, to a certain extent, prevent) musicians from acting intuitively, the activity that is itself being researched.

At this point in the process, the role of the musician and the researcher overlap. Comprehensive observation is possible through the differing perspectives available to each participant. Whilst this appears most feasible when considering a participatory action research scenario – in which the musician and researcher are two different people – the use of video-recording allows a single reflective practitioner to take advantage of multiple perspectives. In addition, musicians could benefit from maintaining in-depth journals of their experiences, providing they have time to do so effectively. Although both video-recorded observation and journal writing would undeniably only capture *post hoc* reflection, their importance in capturing the performer's perspective would be invaluable.

The reflection stage relies most heavily upon the skills and background of the empirical musicologist. Based on observation, the researcher may draw on a consortium of methods from both academic and practitioner perspectives, including interviews with coperformers, case studies and surveys of associated literature. It is important to note that the inspiration of the reflection stage arises from the actions of the musician. Similarly, the musician may assess the conclusions reached by the musicologist, checking their validity against their experience. Thus, all of the empirical research is grounded in practice.

This cycle of action and reflection may yield a variety of outcomes. The most positivistic (although presumably most rare) consequence would be to arrive at a straightforward conclusion to the questions at hand. A more likely result, however, is that there would be no direct conclusions: instead, the research would generate the material needed to instigate further cycles of action and reflection. In part due to its reliance on Mode 2 knowledge, action research embraces the creation of knowledge in a non-linear fashion. Brydon-Miller describes this development of knowledge as a form of relinquishing control over the exact course of subjects, encouraging what she calls 'messes' (2003: 21). This continuous expansion of knowledge provides two additional outcomes. First, the clarification of concepts and contexts through experience allows subsequent planning and acting stages to be modified so as to more directly assess the questions at hand. Second, the cycle of action and reflection may inspire new avenues of inquiry that may not have been considered originally.

Method

Within this research project, I serve as a reflective practitioner, assuming the combined roles of researcher and musician. This method relies upon both my personal background and the context within which this research is conducted. I am an actively performing bass trombonist, involved in a variety of ensembles. During my doctoral studies at Birmingham Conservatoire, I participated in small brass ensembles, trombone choirs, contemporary music ensembles, jazz bands, brass bands, wind bands and symphony orchestras. In addition, I performed with The Supergroup, a mixed improvised ensemble consisting of other doctoral researchers at the Conservatoire. At the University of Alaska and the University of Michigan (institutions at which I have previously studied), I focused on ensemble performance, going so far as to receive a master's degree in chamber music while simultaneously pursuing a master's degree in trombone performance. In addition to my activities as a performer, I have collaborated with ensembles as an external researcher. While at Birmingham Conservatoire I was able not only to participate within ensembles but also to observe a variety of others throughout rehearsals, workshops and performances. In particular, I extensively video-recorded the Boult Quartet, the Conservatoire's most senior postgraduate string quartet.

In addition to practical musical experience, I have been involved in musicological scholarship throughout my postgraduate and doctoral degrees. Of particular interest has been the application of nonmusical research to musicological theories and contexts in an attempt to identify the nature of musical knowledge. This has provided me with a background in sociological research as well as a critical approach to academic research in general. The combination of practical and academic experience enables me to be in an ideal position to serve as reflective practitioner within this project. Recalling the intentions outlined in the preface, this text should not only expand upon the propositional knowledge generated from academic research of musical performance, but allow for theoretical modelling of the procedural knowledge used every day by performers.

At Birmingham Conservatoire, I played in a collection of ensembles for a variety of durations. Long-term placements within ensembles extended between one to three months and included participation in a brass band, symphony orchestras and contemporary groups such as Interrobang and The Supergroup. Short-term placements generally focused on the preparation of a single concert and included jazz ensemble performances and recordings, brass dectet performances and involvement with professional contemporary ensemble Decibel. Singular involvement involved one-off placement within reading orchestras and substituting for other musicians around the Conservatoire on an ad hoc basis. All of these placements provided valuable material and experience upon which I could reflect while simultaneously maintaining my role as an active performer.

My involvement within ensembles was complemented by some of the empirical methodologies discussed previously in this chapter. In working with the Boult Quartet, I observed rehearsals from a first play-through to a polished performance of Samuel Barber's *String Quartet No. 1, Op. 11* (1939). These rehearsals were video-recorded over the span of four days, providing an example of concentrated preparation of a single work. In addition, several rehearsals and performances given by The Supergroup were recorded, allowing for critique and analysis of myself within the environment of a small ensemble. The members of The Supergroup participated in semi-open interviews within rehearsals, allowing me to introduce them to and engage them with critical reflection. Whilst analysis of the

Boult Quartet will be woven throughout the text, the improvisation found within performances by The Supergroup will be examined in detail in Chapter 6.[19]

Underlying my own practice and collaboration with the Boult Quartet and The Supergroup has been an extensive literature review. As will become apparent throughout this text, the academic elements of this research have emerged and been critiqued from a practical perspective due to my ongoing activity as a musician. In this manner, practice informs my reception of academic research, which in turn encourages me to reflect on my practice in new ways.

At the intersection between practical research and academic research lies my reflective journal. In it, I have expanded the examination of my own musical practice to encompass the entire research project. Emphasizing the cyclical aspect of action research, the journal presents a vital cohesive element linking action and reflection. In effect, what originally started as research on musical performance has evolved into research upon research on musical performance – an aspect of what Schön refers to as reflective research (1983: 309). Whilst the journal was never meant for public use, nearly all of the ideas therein have been reformulated into the formal arguments found throughout this book.

Conclusion

Given the extensive discussion of methodological considerations presented in this chapter, it is now possible to turn to the research questions at hand. Critical evaluation of current musicological research on ensemble performance, relevant non-musicological research and musical experience is necessary due to the different forms of knowledge under consideration. Through the investigation of these research questions, deeper epistemological questions may arise, progressing beyond issues surrounding the identification of gestures or how ensembles interact. As will become apparent, ensemble performance may engage musicians in levels of embodied knowledge previously unexplored through propositional or procedural means. This ostensibly hypothetical proposition is reified through exploration of the research questions posed above. Thus, this book provides an examination of a specific kind of Mode 2 knowledge – performative musical knowledge – through the lens of ensemble performance.

---

[19]   The members of these two ensembles have granted their permission to use their likeness and any rehearsal discussion within this book, ensuring that my work conforms with standard research guidelines.

Chapter 2
Beyond Communication

The first of the four research questions I posed in Chapter 1 addresses the processes by which musicians interact and share information with each other while performing. More appropriately, however, this query may be regarded as two separate sub-questions: how do musicians interact while performing? And how do musicians share information while performing? Whilst closely related, the processes of interaction within a group and the dissemination of information are intrinsically different. Understanding of the second sub-question – how musicians share information – necessarily predicates any exploration of how ensembles interact. Consequently, in order to address this second point, a working understanding of the content of the information disseminated needs to be established. Reflecting upon the narrative presented at the beginning of Chapter 1, it can be assumed that the information communicated throughout a musical ensemble must, in some way, pertain to the variables of the musical performance itself: tempo, dynamics, intonation, phrasing and interpretation. Ensemble performance within Western art music requires some if not all of these variables to be coordinated amongst those performing. Attention to these elements is necessary in order to produce a cohesive and compelling performance – one that, some may argue, 'communicates' effectively to the audience. Therein lies the importance of ensemble collaboration. Regardless of whether or not the musicians can 'communicate' something to an audience in the same way a storyteller could, ensemble performance is gauged by the extent to which the participants can coordinate temporally, harmonically, expressively, aesthetically and so on.[1] Consequently, this chapter will focus on determining the ways in which coperformers can communicate these variables with each other. As will become increasingly apparent, this working understanding of the information being shared amongst ensemble members does not express the entirety of the nuances that may be expressed through performance. Further exploration of this topic will take place within the next chapter.

Frederick Seddon identifies that both verbal and nonverbal communication may exist within musical ensembles (2005: 47).[2] Although many researchers have

---

[1] For example, a negative newspaper review of a concert by the Tokyo String Quartet referred to 'disturbing miscalculations of pitch, … ensemble (a shaky pianissimo conclusion to the Tchaikovsky's third movement, and some disagreements in the quick figures of the finale) and style' (Bargreen, 1998).

[2] Whilst Seddon originally mentions a third mode, musical communication, this concept is only passingly delved into through the rest of his 2005 article.

noted that musical rehearsals are broken down into time spent performing and time spent talking, Seddon is the first to consider these two activities in terms of the kind of communication that takes place within them. However, these activities are not balanced either in terms of time devoted to them or the range of actions that constitute them. As remarked previously, several studies have shown that small ensembles tend to spend the majority of rehearsal time playing rather than talking.[3] From my experience observing the Boult Quartet and participating in The Supergroup, I can attest to the disproportionately large amount of time engaged in performance during rehearsal. The categories of verbal and nonverbal communication, although ostensibly evident, are problematic. Although verbal communication has been concretely identified within the realm of human interaction, nonverbal communication has only been identified as communication through exchanges that are not verbal. This classification amalgamates a large collection of seemingly disparate processes, described by Seddon as including 'body language, facial expression, eye contact, musical cues and gesticulations' (2005: 54). Whilst ensuing musicological research has focused on only one or two of these nonverbal activities in turn, the 'nonverbal' classification remains common.[4]

Bearing in mind the mixed use of verbal and nonverbal communication in ensemble interaction, this chapter will explore the primary models of communication currently used in the field of performance studies. These models claim to encompass not only the processes within ensemble interaction but also the relationships between composer, performer and audience – a distinction whose implications may not have been fully realized. Closer examination of these models reveals that they do not adequately account for the complexity of ensemble interaction, thereby requiring an in-depth exploration of the processes by which leadership operates within ensembles. After analysing several examples of a professional level string quartet (the paradigmatic ensemble within Western art music), however, several issues arise regarding how information is actually communicated to ensemble members and the role leadership may or may not play in this sharing of information. More importantly, the ensuing discussions will critique the appropriateness of the communicative paradigm that underlies current theories of ensemble interaction. I propose that musicological research on ensembles has been based upon assumptions about the similarity between ensembles and other social groups – similarities that are easily exaggerated. This discussion will motivate a shift of critical focus from the group to the individual, prompting an investigation of the phenomenology of the solo musician. As will become evident, it is only through an understanding of the phenomenology of solo performance (and the informational content that may emerge from performance) that a new paradigm of ensemble interaction may be proposed.

---

[3]   Blank and Davidson, 2007; Blum, 1987; Seddon and Biasutti, 2009; Tovstiga et al., 2004; and Williamon and Davidson, 2002.

[4]   Ford and Davidson, 2003; Tovstiga et al., 2004; Ginsborg et al., 2006; King, 2006b; Blank and Davidson, 2007; and Broughton and Stevens, 2007, among others.

The Pursuit of Sameness

Before progressing to the body of this chapter, I wish to delineate between two important aspects of social interaction. This distinction is not intended to restrict the discussions that may arise throughout this book: rather, it will clarify the method and intended outcome of my practical and theoretical arguments.[5] Human interaction involves not only the mechanics of cause and effect between individuals' intentions and actions, but also the social and emotional environment that emerges through those mechanics. Whilst the discussions that will take place within this book are mostly mechanically oriented, focusing on the processes by which humans act and react to each other, it is important to bear in mind that ensemble performance has the ability to beget unique emotional relationships between musicians. Through performance, especially performance where the mechanical aspects of interaction have become second nature, musicians may shed the emotional baggage they may begrudge their peers and connect with them on a more fundamental social level. Thomas Turino describes how the interpersonal connection created within ensembles is reliant upon both the process and the product of making music:

> For me, good music making or dancing is a realization of ideal – *possible* – human relationships where the identification with others is so direct and so intense that we feel, for those best moments, as if our selves have merged. It is the sounds we are making, our art, that continually let us know that we have done so or that we are failing to achieve this ideal. (2008: 19)

Notably, Turino remarks that this merging of selves occurs during 'good music making'. Whether this activity is technically good (that is to say, of a high proficiency) and therefore encourages the development of sameness or is ontologically good because of the resulting cathartic sameness is not specified. Regardless, the outcome of 'good music making' is beneficial musically and socially, allowing for the achievement of communitas. This condition, originally proposed by anthropologist Victor Turner, is described by Turino as 'a possible collective state' in which 'personal distinctions are stripped away allowing people to temporarily merge through their basic humanity' (Turino, 2008: 18, referencing Turner, 1969). The sameness that Turino describes within group musical performance may be accessible through various other rituals in everyday life.

In *Music as Social Life: The Politics of Participation* (2008), Turino addresses the social and emotional implications of participating within ensembles. He distinguishes between two types of musical settings that involve live performance (that which is not dependent on the medium of recorded sound): presentational and participatory performance. Presentational performance is created by musicians

---

[5]   I would like to express thanks to Ian Cross for introducing me to ethnomusicological research on social dynamics within ensembles.

(particularly specialists) so that others may listen to it (Ibid.: 52). Alternatively, participatory performance involves anyone who wishes to be involved, resulting in a setting that prioritizes process and any emergent social outcomes rather than a specific sonic output (Ibid.: 28). Turino clarifies the distinction between these musical settings by explaining that presentational performance regards 'a musical piece as a set item, an art object, whereas in participatory music a piece is more like a set of resources, like the rules and stock moves of a game refashioned anew during each performance' (Ibid.: 54). As a result, these approaches engender priorities and results that differ musically and socially. Presentational performance, as can be seen in the development of virtuosic specialist musicians, places an emphasis on sustaining the interest of an audience that is not actively involved in the creation of sonic output. Thus, the music played within presentational contexts is accordingly highly complex and elaborate. Participatory performance does not distinguish between a performer and an audience; there are merely 'participants and potential participants' (Ibid.: 28). Due to both the large numbers of people which may be involved in a performance within this context (and the varying amount of experience using musical instruments), the resulting music is generally compromised of ostensibly simple patterns that develop gradually over the course of a performance.

Whilst Turino clarifies that presentational and participatory performances exist on a continuum (in addition to recorded forms of performance such as high fidelity music and studio audio art), his exploration of these kinds of performance does not examine which social aspects of participatory music may be found within ensemble presentational performance. Within the two types of performance he describes, there is a clear distinction between the relationships between performer and audience. As mentioned previously, however, the interaction between ensemble musicians is of a fundamentally different nature from that between performer and audience. In essence, the research questions addressed throughout this book seek to find the practical mechanisms by which ensembles work in order to encourage the development of social unity. Through this, it may be possible to consider the elements of presentational performance that induce similar social and emotional outcomes within the musicians involved as is normally found within participatory performance.

Models of Communication

To begin, it is necessary to examine how communication has been modelled thus far in performance studies. Drawing heavily upon sociological and psychological literature, this area of performance research attempts to find parallels between social and musical interaction. The first model to be discussed focuses on the application of linguistic models of communication to coperformer interaction. The second model, on the other hand, draws influence not from linguistics but from gestural studies. Examination of each model from the perspective of a reflective musician will highlight issues with the application of nonmusical theories to performance research.

In their research on solo piano performance, Eric Clarke and Jane Davidson describe the models of performance present at the advent of performance studies as too simplistic, portraying the process 'simply as the flow of information from input through a set of abstract expressive rules to an output effector system' (1998: 76). The reality, they go on to say, 'is far more practical and corporeal. The body is not just a source of sensory input and a mechanism for effecting output: it is far more intimately bound up with our whole response to music' (Ibid.: 76). Although the relationship described between the performer's body and expressivity is presented within the context of its effects on audiences, this concept implicitly permeates subsequent research on performance, shifting the emphasis of future operative models towards the physical elements of human interaction. Anthony Gritten and Elaine King, in the introduction to their most recent compendium on music and gesture, note that the work presented in the text is 'grounded in the premise that musical gestures are cross-modal and that gestures include non-sounding physical movements as well as those that produce sound' (2011: 6). Thus, the study of gesture in performance encompasses a wide range of human experience.

Given that research on interaction within ensembles focuses on musicians' physical gestures, it is necessary to explore the visible elements of performance itself. Performing acoustic music is inherently physical and constituent motions may fulfil any number of functions. Elaine King and Jane Ginsborg, in their research on solo vocalists and accompanists within Western art music, comment that bodily gestures function in two manners: 'enabling the performer actually to produce sound, technically realising the notes contained in a musical score' and 'achieving and conveying an expressive effect' (2011: 179). Along the same lines, Alexander Jensenius et al. further discriminate between the movements made during performance, dividing them into the following categories:

- Sound-producing gestures: 'those that effectively produce sound[,] further subdivided into gestures of excitation and modification'.
- Communicative gestures: those 'intended mainly for communication[,] subdivided into performer–performer or performer–perceiver types'.
- Sound-facilitating gestures: those that 'support the sound-producing gestures[,] subdivided into support, phrasing, and entrained gestures'.
- Sound-accompanying gestures: those 'not involved in the sound production itself, but follow the music. They can be sound-tracing … or they can mimic the sound-producing gestures'. (2010: 23)

Whilst previous research on physical motion in performance focuses exclusively on communicative gestures,[6] it is important to note that the classifications proposed

---

[6]   Blank and Davidson, 2007; Clarke and Davidson, 1998; Davidson, 2001, 2002, 2006; Davidson and King, 2004; King and Ginsborg, 2011; and Seddon and Biasutti, 2009.

by Jensenius incorporates this category as *independent* of the other motions in musical performance. Even so, the authors retain the possibility that all actions executed in performance are communicative in some way. In distinguishing communicative gestures from the other categories, the authors propose that:

> all performance movements can be considered a type of communication, but we find it useful to have a separate category for movements that are primarily intended to be communicative. These may be performer–performer or performer–perceiver types of communication, and range from communication in a linguistic sense (emblems) to a more abstract form of communication. (Jensenius et al., 2010: 25)

The authors' last statement about the range of communicative possibilities raises questions regarding the nature of communication itself, particularly how communication may be considered 'abstract'. Further examination of this topic will be discussed later in this chapter.

Before continuing, it is important to clarify the terminology used throughout this research. Marc Leman and Rolf Godøy, in the introduction to *Musical Gestures: Sound, Movement, and Meaning*, describe a gesture as a movement that 'in some way [acts as] a carrier of expression and meaning' (2010: 5). Whilst any physical motion through space may be considered a movement, a gesture is imbued with some amount of significance. That significance may be to 'control the musical instrument when playing a melodic figure, to coordinate actions among musicians (conducting gestures), or to impress an audience (for example, moving the head during a solo performance)' (Ibid.: 5). Jensenius et al. clarify this definition, commenting that the term gesture 'does not refer to body movement or expression *per se*, but rather to the intended or perceived meaning of the movement or expression' (2010: 15). The perceiver therefore plays an important role in the determination and reception of gestures.

The Linguistic Model of Communication

The first model of communication to be considered is dependent upon correlating the informational content of physical gestures with that of speech. Building on the corpus of previous research on gesture in nonmusical social interaction such as David McNeill's work on gesture in speech,[7] Clarke and Davidson suggest that solo musicians intend that their physical actions carry expressive meaning in performance. They propose that 'gestural repertoires emerge which are associated with specific meanings, and it seems to be the case that performers … develop specific gestures for particular expressive purposes – a gestural movement repertoire' (1998: 80). Although the emphasis of this statement is on the existence of gestural repertoires, it is important to note the authors' use of the phrase 'specific

---

[7]   For examples of this literature, see McNeill, 2000.

meanings'. Through this, Clarke and Davidson identify gesture as a referential tool. From this perspective, the physical actions of performers themselves become a medium by which meaning (informational or emotional) can be communicated to an audience. Davidson's next study further explores the idea of physical gesture as expression. Drawing on categories proposed by behaviourists Paul Ekman and Wallace Friesen – adaptive, regulatory and illustrative/emblematic – she attempts to identify gestures in a performance of Annie Lennox (Davidson, 2001: 242, citing Ekman and Friesen, 1969). Davidson theorizes that these gestures provide clues about the meaning of the song being performed, allowing for clarification of the lyrics and the narrative presented to the audience (2001: 244). She argues that performers' gestures can and should be used by audiences as another medium of interpretation in addition to sound, recalling Nicholas Cook's thesis[8] that performance is a multimedia event (Ibid.: 250). This raises several issues about the relationship between gesture and music as well as the substantial problems surrounding the identification of musical meaning.

Throughout her research, Davidson posits that physical gestures in musical performance are both intentionally meaningful and necessary to provide a complete artistic experience for the audience. Whilst the first of these assumptions may hold true for dance, dramatics and musical theatre, its validity in Western classical music is partial at best. Notwithstanding opera and other mixed media genres, the primary physical manifestation of music is sound (Johnson, 2002). This is evidenced by the presence of a flourishing recording industry whose output is, above all, compact discs and digital audio files.[9] With her conclusion that musical performance is a multimedia event, Davidson implies that if one does not experience one medium of the performance (visual, in particular) one does not fully experience the musical work. In later writings, she tempers this assertion, stating 'of course, performers do not have to be seen in order to be understood, but the significance of visual cues cannot be underestimated' (2005: 234). That said, Davidson continues to assert that audiences can draw upon performers' actions as a primary source of musical meaning and information. The idea that physical gestures are intentionally meaningful to an audience, however, seems more appropriate to theatrical performance than musical. In musical performance (particularly in Western art music), there are many actions that a performer carries out that, although necessary to the production of the music, do not have any bearing on what the audience is intended to perceive. As a bass trombonist, for example, I have to periodically empty moisture from my instrument. In order to do so, I drastically change the position of the instrument in relation to my body – much more so than I would while playing. However, that action is not intended to carry any significant meaning to the audience. Even if an audience member

---

8   From Cook, 2000.

9   Whilst the viability of audio recordings as musical artefacts is still debated, further discussion of this aspect of performance is beyond the scope of this book. For more information, see Bayley, 2009.

were reading every movement I make in an effort to discern clues to my overall interpretation of a piece (if that is what a listener actually does), the only thing that could realistically be signified by the emptying of my spit valve is that my instrument has too much condensation.[10] Audiences familiar with live performance will disregard such actions. One could envision a similar case during a rock concert: when a guitarist presses their foot on a distortion pedal, their action could only realistically be interpreted as an intermediary act. The motion itself, whilst necessary to the musical performance, is not ostensibly expressive or meaningful. This does not necessarily mean that gestures cannot be used as expressive tools by performers; vocalists from classical and popular music backgrounds, as Davidson has shown, are commonly taught to display emotion through facial expression and body language. Rather, there exists a range of gestures that are not intended for audience consumption. This is particularly the case when examining performances involving more than one musician. Although Davidson's research focuses almost exclusively on solo pianists and pop vocalists, these specific situations are not representative of the practices found in Western art or popular music in general.

At a deeper level, Davidson's research evades the problems surrounding notions of meaning in music. Found throughout these two studies and her subsequent research are references to music having 'specific meanings' (Clarke and Davidson, 1998), 'musical "messages"' (Davidson, 2001) and musical communication (Davidson, 2002, 2006, 2012; Williamon and Davidson, 2002). If such communication exists between a performer and their audience, what is being communicated? Ian Cross addresses this question in his critique of the communication model used in information theory (2005: 30). He finds the process of a sender transmitting information to a receiver – who is then required to decode the information – to be unsatisfactory in that 'the meaning or significance of musical behaviour or of a piece of music can rarely be pinned down unambiguously' (Ibid.: 30). This ambiguity is somewhat contrary to the way language is assumed to operate in post-Enlightenment discourses, where words are taken to function as referents to concepts or ideas. Even the most metaphorical language still references something else, a concept that will be applied to language about music later in this book. Whilst the post-structural concept of language developed by philosophers such as Derrida and Foucault identifies language as being inherently self-referential, the reflexive nature of music seems to be of a much higher degree than that of language, resulting in considerably more ambiguity. Kofi Agawu thus argues that music, while similar to language in several ways, does not have a 'more or less fixed lexical meaning' (2009: 25). This sentiment is echoed by Albrecht Schneider, who comments that music can be 'compared to (natural) languages in respect to grammatical and syntactic categories fairly well. Music differs most, though, from (natural) languages with respect to semantics as music

---

[10]   It is not outside of the realm of possibility that a composer may use the motion of emptying a spit valve within a composition, particularly in performance art. However, the action would most likely not be interpreted as a meaningful gesture by the audience.

normally is lacking a lexicon of words that denote a certain meaning' (2010: 79). Similarly, Peter Kivy remarks that whilst 'music is ... language-like in certain respects, it is not language; it is not a language or part of a language' (2007: 214). Davidson, however, appears to conflate musical and linguistic meaning. In her research on pop musicians Annie Lennox and Robbie Williams, she maintains that physical gestures add a layer of information (described as 'musical expression') to that being delivered to the audience through the lyrics of the songs being performed (Davidson, 2002: 145 and Davidson, 2006). What the author actually describes in these cases is the relationship between the lyrics and the gestures used. This proposal echoes research by psychologists Cassell and McNeill, who propose that storytellers communicate different narrativic levels through the use of gestures (1991). Although Davidson's work may corroborate with this field of psychological research, it does not directly address the relationship between performers' gestures and the musical content itself. Therefore, I hesitate to describe the information expressed through performers' gestures in this manner as 'musical'.

The Gestural Model of Communication

As opposed to the linguistic model of communication in performance, the gestural model does not attempt to match gestures with lexical correlates. This is in part due to the emphasis the gestural model of communication places upon instrumental performance. Whilst researchers such as Davidson, King and Ginsborg have applied linguistic models of communication when analysing jazz, pop and classical vocalists,[11] the possibility that physical gestures in performance are intrinsically associated with lyrics is not applicable to instrumental music. It is from this dilemma that a different model has been presented. Ole Kühl proposes a semiotic approach to understanding the relationship between expression and music in general, writing that whilst 'musical meaning cannot be pinpointed in any specified manner[,] the most important, stable element in a musical semantics is the primary signification from musical phrase to gesture and from musical gesture to emotional content' (2011: 129). This is reminiscent of Peter Elsdon's work on solo piano performances by Keith Jarrett (2006). In this research he concentrates on finding a broader understanding of the use of instrumentalists' gestures, rather than pinpointing specific gestures or analogous meanings. Elsdon's conclusions are accordingly broad: 'for the viewer the physical behaviours of the performing body are understood as manifestations of something unseen; to put it differently, bodily gestures are taken to represent interior mental states' (Ibid.: 200). This statement, whilst seemingly straightforward, indirectly addresses the audience's perception of authorship. The 'interior mental states' Elsdon refers to are undoubtedly those of the performer, as the performer's actions are being taken as representations of them. Are the performer's mental or emotional states, then, an integral part of the musical work? If so, then many a wedding performance of Pachelbel's *Canon in D*

---

[11]   See Davidson, 2005, 2006; and King and Ginsborg, 2011, respectively.

may only express boredom. Revising Elsdon's conclusion to refer to '*perceived interior mental states*' may, therefore, more accurately represent the role of the audience in this process.

Both models of communication carry the implication that the content being conveyed to the audience is primarily of an emotional nature. Davidson's work in particular has inspired further research on the importance of the visual when gauging perceived emotionality within musicians' performances.[12] However, the relationship between solo performer and audience is markedly different from that found between musicians within an ensemble. Whilst the feedback from an audience does directly affect a musician's unfolding performance, coperformers need to synchronize and execute their parts in such a way as to present a cohesive musical work.[13] The combined simultaneous performances of the musicians involved may then consequently convey emotional content to an audience. Whilst there are countless ongoing debates on the nature of musical meaning and its enigmatic relationship to human emotion, this book must be limited to the investigation of the informational content that may be disseminated between fellow musicians, particularly in regards to performance variables such as tempo, dynamics, intonation, phrasing and interpretation. Consequently, research on gesture in solo performance is markedly different to that on gesture within ensembles due to the fundamental difference of content with which each is concerned. More recent research, whilst recognizing the distinction between these two models of communication, has yet to propose a viable alternative to address the dissemination of information amongst coperformers. Although Jensenius et al. recognize the difference between these two models of communication, describing communicative gestures as ranging from 'communication in a linguistic sense (emblems) to a more abstract form of communication' (2010: 25), the authors do not further examine the validity of these models.

Whilst these models may provide the basis for understanding the relationship between solo performer and audience, they do not adequately address the kind of information that must be communicated between coperformers. For that reason, it is necessary to re-examine the ways that chamber ensemble performers decide upon and share qualitative musical information. Therefore, the next section will examine the notion of leadership within ensembles in an effort to understand how musical variables are agreed upon and disseminated amongst the ensemble members. Through this process, it will be possible to construct a new model of communication that recognizes the unique musical content shared between performers.

---

[12]   For the original research, see Davidson, 1993. For an example of ensuing work, refer to Vines et al., 2005.

[13]   Lutenist Anthony Rooley proposes that audiences provide feedback in the form of 'energy' to the performer, creating a 'wonderful energy transformation' (1990: 41). Although he presents this argument informally, the feedback loops Rooley describes do capture an element of performance that may evade empirical research.

The Case of Leadership

Musicological research on ensemble interaction has drawn heavily upon the fields of psychology and sociology. The first such effort was conducted by social psychologists Vivienne Young and Andrew Colman, in which they describe the inner social workings of string quartets (1979). Two primary themes emerge from their writing: the effects of conflicting interpretative ideas upon ensembles and the amount of centralized leadership necessary for efficient group function (Ibid.: 13, 15). These topics provide the basis upon which more recent research has addressed ensemble studies. Therefore, the following section will not only explore the potential effects of interpretative discrepancies within ensembles, but also the enigmatic concept of musical leadership.

When preparing for performance, musicians have to make decisions regarding how they should interpret the music given them, be it in the form of a score, lead sheet or some other form of internal or external instruction. Arising from the notational gap that occurs when attempting to graphically depict sonic events, these decisions generally deal with matters of style or subjective preference, allowing musicians to choose from a range of theoretically viable alternatives. The rationale for these decisions could be based on a variety of sources, ranging from scholarly research about the musical work, composition or genre, to intuition and personal preference (Hellaby, 2009). When performers are combined in an ensemble, their personal decisions often come into conflict with each other – conflict that can have profound effects upon the operation of the ensemble itself.

Disagreement about interpretation within string quartets has been further researched by Keith Murnighan and Donald Conlon, who designate the phenomenon as 'the Conflict Paradox' (1991: 170). They describe coperformer interaction within Western art music as a fine balance between gridlocking conflict and cooperative mediocrity. Whilst interpretational conflict encourages the growth of interpersonal tension within groups, it sparks creativity and inspires individual freedom. Cooperation, on the other hand, lessens overall interpersonal tension at the risk of incurring blandness in the resulting performance. After surveying professional British string quartets, the authors conclude that successful ensembles ('successful', in this instance, being defined as an assessment of the quartets' concert fees, number of albums and concerts, number of reviews and so on) tend to embrace conflict, preferring the risk of instability over mediocrity (Ibid.: 177).

Use of the term 'conflict', however, might imply a stronger negative connotation than what actually happens within ensemble interaction. For example, when describing his approach to individual interpretational perspectives within the Guarneri String Quartet, violinist Arnold Steinhardt prefers to say that his coperformers 'complement and challenge one another' (Blum, 1987: 5). The positive aspects of challenging situations are further emphasized by Tovstiga et al. in their work with the Carmina Quartet (2004). Through interviews, case studies and observation, the authors conclude that innovation occurs 'in the border region between stability and instability' (Ibid.: 10). Whilst musicians acknowledge the tension created by the conflict paradox, they do not necessarily feel encumbered or overly preoccupied with it in daily rehearsal and performance (Ibid.: 10). Thus, the presentation and exploration of possible interpretations serve as integral elements of creative practice within small ensembles.

Murnighan and Conlon's distillation of ensemble interaction into two possible results – unproductive conflict or insipid cooperation – may be an oversimplification of what is, in reality, a nuanced progression between two extremes. Given the wealth of members' interpretative ideas, ensembles could instead be balanced between the unique input provided by individual members and mutually agreeable parameters. This condition is known as team cognition, 'an emergent state that refers to the manner in which knowledge important to team functioning is mentally organized, represented, and distributed within the team, [allowing] team members to anticipate and execute actions' (DeChurch and Mesmer-Magnus, 2010: 33). Here, organization is balanced between 'knowledge that is distributed among team members (transactive memory)' and 'knowledge that is ... held in common' (Ibid.: 33). Whilst correlating the concept of team cognition to ensemble interaction shows promise, relating these two situations to each other raises more questions than answers. To directly apply this condition to music, one would have to determine the nature of 'musical knowledge' itself, as well as how knowledge and its methods of distribution operate in musical contexts. Such an interdisciplinary correlation may not prove to be as easy as it might first appear. Recalling the distinction between Mode 1 and Mode 2 knowledge, the nature of musical knowledge itself must be discerned before viable comparisons can be made to other fields. This topic, to be addressed within relevant contexts throughout this text, will prove to be vital to constructing a new framework of ensemble interaction. As will become apparent, differences between musical interaction and other forms of social interaction may turn out to be more fundamental than previously considered. Closer examination of leadership within ensembles highlights this discrepancy.

The next section begins by exploring the developmental context for leadership: the circumstantial catalysts that may encourage one or more ensemble members to control the development of a group's performances. From there, I will examine the ways in which leadership may be expressed within ensembles. First will be the application of sociological models of leadership in their most direct application to a musical context – those instances where the musicians are not playing their instruments. Somewhat more complex, however, is the task of unravelling how leadership may operate during performance itself.[14] To do so, I will investigate the expression of leadership in two other specific manners: its expression through physical gesture in performance, as well as leadership by example. These discussions raise important questions regarding the nature of the musical content being expressed by performers and will force us to directly engage with their unique form of Mode 2 knowledge.

---

[14]   Again, my use of 'performance' refers to situations where musicians are actively engaged in playing a piece of music, with or without an audience.

Developmental Contexts for Leadership

In order to understand leadership within ensembles, it is necessary to identify the ways individual musicians may assume positions of power. In her work with undergraduate music students, Elaine King suggests that fixed, personal tendencies predispose certain members towards leadership (2006b). The importance of charisma in the determination of leadership may be found in most (if not all) kinds of social groups (Belbin, 1993). However, King does not account for three other factors that arguably play roles in the determination of leadership: experience, context and the music itself. Experiential leadership may emerge from a discrepancy between skill levels and experience of musicians, encouraging one to assume a pedagogic role. Contextual leadership is based upon the social circumstances of the performance itself: should a performance be at the behest of a particular musician, then they may hold more influence. Musical leadership, on the other hand, emerges from the parameters of the music being played.

In addition to charismatic influences on leadership described previously, the impact of musical experience on leadership should not be underestimated. Each ensemble member has unique experiences and specialities originating from their particular backgrounds. In pedagogical situations where one musician is more proficient than their coperformers, the correlation between experience and leadership is evident. More experienced musicians may fulfil an advisory position due to their practical knowledge. From this perspective, King's observations of the emergence of student leaders could be based both upon charisma and experience. However, professional ensembles do not tend to have such discrepancies in skill level (Turino, 2008: 54). In these circumstances, each member's unique musical background or specialist field may be drawn upon instead. For example, issues arising in the rehearsal of a jazz piece by non-jazz musicians might be referred to the member(s) of the ensemble with the most pertinent experience. Thus, performers' individuality may benefit ensembles.

Social context may also help determine leadership. Performances, especially by students, may be motivated by one particular member. In these situations, the musician whom the performance impacts on most may exert more control. For example, the brass quintet I played in throughout my postgraduate degrees would often perform in members' individual recitals. The main performer received artistic licence for their programmed works as they would be most affected by their performance. In the case of performances featuring the quintet as a whole, this leadership was non-existent. Aside from student ensembles, this form of leadership may also occur in professional contexts, where the public leader of a group (or the artist the other musicians play behind) holds a form of executive power. Neither the Boult Quartet nor The Supergroup, the two primary ensembles I observed at Birmingham Conservatoire, displayed this form of leadership, as the rehearsals and performances observed were on behalf of the entire ensemble.

These two factors affecting the emergence of leaders within ensembles could be considered to be performer-centric, arising through the actions and backgrounds of individual performers. However, musical context also influences who may hold artistic control. This leadership is based on either of two factors: specific pieces' orchestration and cultural convention. In the first instance, the instrument playing the primary line may direct the ensemble's interpretation due to their musical importance.[15] For example, the melody within a jazz group is often referred to as the 'lead', the title implying an associated assumption of power. Likewise, other forms of leadership which are musically based may include a secure rhythmic drive from drums or bass.

An example of musical leadership is demonstrated in an extract from a rehearsal by the Boult Quartet. In the third movement of Barber's *String Quartet No. 1*, bars 41–46, the violist has what the quartet agrees to be the melody. As seen in Video Example 2.1, she complains after a play-through that 'it just sounds too stupid to [play my part at that tempo] (*violist plays excerpt*) – it feels too fast'. Her opinion of the excerpt's tempo is based on what her part is doing in those bars. To substantiate her argument, the violist plays what the resulting melodic line would sound like in context, isolating the specific musical element in question. Therefore, her interpretation is informed by her experience of playing that excerpt within the quartet. In this way, musical context may inspire a performer to encourage a specific shared interpretation with the rest of the ensemble.

In addition to this context-driven musical leadership, there is a strong tradition of conventional instrumental relationships in ensembles. Within standard Western classical ensembles such as a string quartet or brass or wind quintet, the first violin, trumpet or flute are often given more credence in decision-making processes (Norton, 1925: 15). Whilst this does not necessarily grant *carte blanche* authority to their performers, it does imply specific responsibilities. This may be an extension of roles in orchestral situations, where such performers would be the principal musician of their instrumental group. For example, it is not uncommon for a leader to decide upon bowing for a *tutti* string section, or the principal trumpet to determine phrasing to be used throughout the brass. Although a correlation between leadership within chamber ensembles and orchestral sections is possible, investigation of it lies outside of the realm of this book.

The four situational motivations for leadership development described above (charismatic, experiential, contextual and musical) can arise in various degrees and combinations based on circumstance and the musicians involved. Given this, the balance and stability of roles acquired should have an effect upon ensemble interaction. From my experience in a multitude of ensembles, I have witnessed varying balances of power due to circumstance and member composition. At one end of the spectrum is rigid hierarchy: set leadership assumed by specific musicians. This may occur in an ensemble fronted by a well-known musician or in a pedagogical situation. At the other end of the spectrum is a balanced distribution of power, where all members contribute equally toward the direction of the

---

[15]   Ford and Davidson, 2003: 63; Murnighan and Conlon, 1991: 166; and Tovstiga et al., 2004: 10.

group. Whereas formal hierarchy is characterized by its evident leadership, mixed leadership is supremely collaborative.

Leadership Asserted Verbally

Given that ensembles involve both conflict and cooperation, a balance of the two may be maintained through the assertion of leadership. Musicological studies on leadership and group roles within ensembles have drawn extensively from business management research. In order to critique research on leadership within ensembles, however, it is important to briefly compare this body of literature with its non-musicological underpinnings. It is worth noting that this research tends to apply to contexts in which ensembles are not currently playing. However, as mentioned previously, most rehearsal time is devoted to non-linguistic interaction. Drawing from James Burns's seminal work *Leadership* (1978), business management research has divided leadership into two categories: transactional and transformational (Felfe et al., 2004: 266). Additionally, recent research has further identified a third category known as alternating leadership (Andert et al., 2011: 54). Examination of these categories and their characteristics will enable comparison to ensembles, allowing for clarity in determining how applicable such sociological concepts may be to musical interaction.

Transactional leadership emphasizes a causal method of motivation: followers' good performance begets positive reinforcement whilst bad performance encourages the opposite. These leaders 'emphasize goal setting, give instructions, clarify structures and conditions, and take control' and could be considered reactionary (Ibid.: 266). If a certain goal is achieved, the follower is rewarded. If that goal is not achieved, however, the follower requires instruction or more structure.

In contrast, transformational leadership emphasizes followers' personal development. Instead of critiquing followers' actions, transformational leaders focus on 'addressing and modifying their subordinates' values and self esteem, [encouraging them to] go beyond egoistic interests' (Felfe et al., 2004: 266). This depends on four strategies: idealized influence, inspirational motivation, intellectual stimulation and individualized consideration (Ibid.: 267). As these strategies are follower-centric, actions taken to adhere to them are accordingly idiosyncratic.

As opposed to transactional and transformational leadership, alternating leadership eschews a strict hierarchy between leaders and followers. In this model, group members assume '*ad hoc* leadership positions in an intrepreneurial[16] manner by temporarily and freely [alternating] back to be observers, followers, and so forth' (Andert et al., 2011: 54). This results in situations where leadership becomes 'distributed across multiple team members rather than arising from a single, formal leader' (Carson et al., 2007: 1217). Whilst this framework has been

---

[16] 'Intrepreneur' is a neologism combining the prefix 'intra-' and the noun 'entrepreneur'. Andert et al. describe this kind of business figure as a corporate manager 'with a flair for innovation' (2011: 54).

primarily applied to corporations, its similarities to the leadership patterns found within musical ensembles are unmistakeable, making it tempting to correlate the two. Through a series of surveys, Avi Gilboa and Malka Tal-Shmotkin successfully draw comparisons between perceived trends in leadership and interaction within string quartets and self-managed teams (2012). However, research on alternating leadership has not specified the qualities participants display in this model beyond noting that they are distinct from the characteristics of observers or followers. Likewise, Gilboa and Tal-Shmotkin do not progress beyond recognizing that musicians tend to associate the qualities used within string quartet performance with those in self-managed teams. Therefore, additional comparison to the activities of musicians within ensembles would be pre-emptive.

Elements of transactional and transformational leadership are found in the work of Elaine King, who describes and categorizes the team roles observed within undergraduate student ensembles (2006b). She identifies a charismatic development of leadership, originally proposed by management theorist Meredith Belbin. As happens in any social situation, people tend towards leadership roles based on their personality (Belbin, 1993: 32). This predisposition allows musicians to control ensembles in situations that might lack compelling motivation from other sources. The leadership exhibited in King's research is more transactional than transformational, as she notes that the leader was generally of higher technical level than their coperformers. Whilst she does not identify specific leadership characteristics, King concludes that the establishment of a leader is critical to an ensemble's success (2006b: 279).

Contrary to King's research, Mariana Manduell and Alan Wing describe how professional flamenco ensembles exhibit highly flexible forms of leadership:

> There is some form of (shifting) leadership during most of a performance, but as long as ensemble members do not compromise the performance, they have a fair amount of freedom ... Roles change, and it is sometimes difficult to place oneself within the hierarchy of command. Confrontations do occur, as do compromises, but management seems to be more of an 'accommodation' between ensemble members rather than either of the two extremes. (2007: 613)

Leadership in this context is more fluid than transactional or transformational models, as performers spontaneously contribute to the ensemble's artistic direction. These contributions are vitally important not only to the immediate performance aesthetic of the ensemble, but also to individual performers' morale and involvement (see Tovstiga et al., 2004: 10). From a sociological perspective, this form of ensemble leadership is similar to alternating leadership.

Contradiction over the kind of leadership necessary for ensembles originates from a fundamental difference between the groups investigated. Younger ensembles, such as those observed by King, may benefit from stricter guidelines; fixed hierarchies could effectively mould nascent groups into functioning units, allowing these musicians to develop individual responsibility. Flexible leadership, as exhibited by professional ensembles, encourages creativity and innovation without compromising the group's cohesion and productivity (see Blum, 1987 and Tovstiga et al., 2004). The necessity of distinct hierarchies appears to be characteristic of less mature ensembles, whereas more experienced ensembles do not require formal leadership.

Even where leadership is defined, the use of contributions from each ensemble member is valuable to group morale. Davidson and King comment that 'it is important that every voice is heard [in rehearsals]' so that 'every individual participant [feels] that he or she can contribute as desired' (2004: 107). This echoes sociologist Tom Douglas's comment that 'nothing causes people in any organization to feel redundant quicker than to realize that all the important decisions in their group life are made by others' (1978: 50). Whilst this conclusion is drawn from Douglas's observation of nonmusical groups, musicological research confirms its applicability to ensembles. Yaakov Atik concludes that occupational stress on orchestral musicians may come from two sources (1994). First, many members of a symphony have an ostensibly redundant job role. Particularly in the string sections, there may be a dozen or more people playing the same part.[17] Second, conductors may inhibit musicians' feelings of individual creativity, due to their presumed omnipotent directorial position. Atik concludes that these working conditions could result in 'long-term costs in terms of motivation and career aspirations' (Ibid.: 22). Thus, contributions from all members of an ensemble are necessary for its creative atmosphere and healthy morale, regardless of flexibility of leadership.

Leadership through Physical Gesture

Given that small ensembles may exhibit elements of transactional, transformational and alternating leadership, it is important to recall that verbally articulated leadership is only an part of a larger picture. Therefore, it is necessary to examine leadership tendencies within performance. Research on the use of physical gestures within ensembles emerges from literature on audiences' perception of performance gestures. Beyond addressing issues arising in solo performance (the meaning, if any, of gestures and the possibility of gestural repertoires), social interaction has to be taken into consideration. The following section will examine how communicative gestures may enable efficient and effective group interaction. Several common features have emerged from research in this area, falling into three categories: cueing systems, visual contact, and physical gestures as indicative of interpretation. Discussion of these topics seldom occur individually, as each plays an important role in the overarching performative interactions of musicians.

---

[17]   As a brass player, I am more familiar with a different form of redundancy: that of performing in a concert where I may only play one movement out of several larger orchestral works.

Research on cueing systems extends studies on synchronization between musicians which have focused primarily on the timing and coordination of sound. Building on the pioneering work of Rudolf Rasch (1979 and 1988), more recent research shifts from temporal and sonic aspects of synchronization to the social. King explores ways that coperformer synchrony may be achieved, concluding that the processes of 'hunting' and 'cooperating' allow groups to maintain the 'illusion of perfect ensemble' (Goodman, 2002: 155). Manduell and Wing approach the issue differently, proposing that ensemble members act more like components of a connected network than individuals (2007). Although useful, research on synchronization is limited to the coordination of tempi to the exclusion of other variables such as volume, timbre, articulation, expression and so on. As these other qualities play a large role in determining the cohesiveness of an ensemble, conclusions from this research are incomplete. From my experience playing in small ensembles (and even with larger band and orchestral sections), the difficulties arising from unmatched timbre or articulation often rival those resulting from unstable tempi. Beyond the research thus far discussed, musicological literature specifies little else about cues other than that they exist primarily at entrances, exits and other structurally important points in music (Williamon and Davidson, 2002). This lack of specificity could result from the variety of ways musicians interact with their particular instruments, an area that has not been explicitly studied outside of pedagogical literature. Musicians' actions are necessarily affected by the instrument they play, just as athletes move differently depending on their physiology and the sport they play. Therefore, although cues may contain common features, there may not exist a single formula for understanding how they are created. As superficial physical characteristics may be different, they may serve instead as caricatures for shared musical concepts.

Whilst cues are used intentionally in small ensemble interaction to benefit ensemble coordination, questions arise as to who is meant to see and gain information from them. Davidson and King maintain that conscious gestures should be used in order to establish 'an effective three-way communication between [the performer], the ensemble, and the audience' (2004: 113). However, Manduell and Wing remind us that ensemble performance requires gestures noticeable to coperformers yet invisible to an audience. They write that 'the focal performer [of a flamenco group], who has the primary responsibility for cueing, must ensure during the performance that the cues are subtle enough not to attract (distract) audience attention yet are obvious enough to the ensemble to be recognized during the performance despite other distractions' (Manduell and Wing, 2007: 611). Violinist Arnold Steinhardt comments that although cues are necessary in non-conducted ensembles, 'it's important not to allow our gestures to distract from the line of the music. Whether we like it or not, the audience takes in the visual aspect as part of the experience' (Blum, 1987: 10). This suggests that as different forms of perception are used by the audience and coperformers, certain gestures are appropriate for specific intended receivers. From my experience within ensembles, there is a tacit understanding that cues can become 'too big' and overly noticeable. Likewise, excessive tapping of feet, a habit with both visual and aural consequences, is generally avoided in current performance practice of Western classical music. These actions can distract an audience, prompting the (probably unrealistic, yet nevertheless present) fear that an audience may become preoccupied with the way musicians look rather than how they sound.

Visual contact between performers is the passive counterpart to cueing systems. Its use in ensembles has been identified as vitally important to group cohesion throughout the field's collected body of literature.[18] However, research is divided on exactly what kind of visual contact is beneficial. Aaron Williamon and Jane Davidson stress the importance of direct eye contact based on their observations of piano duos (2002). This emphasis continues in subsequent research conducted by Davidson herself, King, Ford and Ginsborg, who propose that performers should focus less on each others' eyes and more on the rest of their bodies.[19] Williamon and Davidson remark that 'looking was not simply a result of observing one another's hands, facial expression and so on, but rather a process for sharing ideas' (2002: 62). That being said, the authors still conclude that eye contact establishes a relationship through which ideas are shared.[20] On the other hand, the Guarneri Quartet reveal that they avoid direct eye contact: visual contact focuses on their coperformers' fingers (Blum, 1987: 14). This, alongside research on choral ensembles by Liz Garnett (2009), implies that performers may not necessarily receive information through each others' eyes. Instead, eye contact may be more important in establishing the intimate relationship necessary in order to enter a shared performance environment. Subsequently, qualitative information about the music itself may arise from observations of performers' physical gestures, regardless of any intended communication.

Performers' body language may also provide insight into their intended musical expression and character. Williamon and Davidson argue that the human body is the 'physical centre for expressive information' (2002: 44). King and Ginsborg, paraphrasing one aspect of Davidson's position, propose that singers' characters can be expressed through their gestures (2011: 180). Similar to how people understand and correctly interpret their friends' body language, musicians' awareness of their coperformers' idiosyncratic movements heightens over prolonged periods of time. Therefore, as performers work together, they become attuned to each others' body language and ways of playing their instruments (Blum, 1987: 14). Just as individual gestures may be used to achieve certain goals

---

[18]   Blum, 1987; Davidson and Good, 2002; Ford and Davidson, 2003; Leman, 2010; Tovstiga et al., 2004; and Williamon and Davidson, 2002, among others.

[19]   Davidson and King, 2004; Ford and Davidson, 2003; and King and Ginsborg, 2011.

[20]   The content of the ideas being shared is never explicitly stated, although the authors comment that 'the observed [torso] swaying could represent the global level in a hierarchy of expressive gestural information, with the hands providing a local indicator' (Williamon and Davidson, 2002: 64). Upon reflection, however, this description does not clarify what information is being shared, other than that it is gestural in nature.

(as is the case with cues), body language may be manipulated. There is, however, an important distinction in what is conveyed through each. Whilst cues address the question of *when* to play, body language may address the question of *how* to play. King alludes to this in relation to conducting, commenting that 'the conductor communicates much more than just a beat, for the members of an orchestra might read visual signals about expression through a conductor's entire body language in the same way that the coperformers of a string quartet might project interpretative ideas by watching each other's physical movements' (Goodman, 2002: 159). Williamon and Davidson additionally mention gesture as a source of information about performance intention (2002: 55). Subsequent literature, however, focuses on the effect of gesture and body language on coordination of timing rather than coordination of interpretation.[21] Likewise, this research strives to generate a taxonomy of gestures rather than investigate how those gestures may disseminate qualitative musical information. Whilst this literature confirms that there is some form of leadership taking place through cues, eye contact and body language, it simply affirms its existence without examining any underlying processes.

Leadership by Example

Given that musical leadership may be articulated through language and physical gesture, may performance itself express leadership? The following discussion examines how sociological models of leadership may operate in nonverbal environments, highlighting how musicians exert influence simply by performing in a certain manner. As mentioned earlier, alternating leadership is defined by the leadership each group member expresses over time rather than a set of characteristics, limiting its direct application to musical contexts. Therefore, this section will attempt to apply just transactional and transformational leadership models to unconducted ensemble performance.

Recalling the characteristics of transactional leadership (setting goals, giving instructions, clarifying structures and taking control), are any present within ensemble performance?[22] 'Goal setting' is ambiguous due to issues defining what musical goals are. Theoretically, an ensemble's goal could be to produce a contextually successful performance. However, is it possible to set goals while playing music itself? In addition to basic parameters such as tempo and volume, more abstract concepts such as expressively or in a certain style can be 'set' by musicians, encouraging coperformers to attain or maintain target parameters. Even if specific qualities are difficult to verbalize, these concepts are common within ensemble rehearsal. By performing within these parameters, musicians may lead by example, 'clarifying structures and conditions'. 'Giving instructions' could be interpreted similarly; one musician may demonstrate a certain passage to their peers through performance. Thus, a musician can effectively 'take control', regulating

---

21   Ford and Davidson, 2003; Davidson and King, 2004; and Manduell and Wing, 2007.
22   For consideration of this question in terms of conducted ensembles, see Atik, 1994.

how the performance should sound. John Sloboda alludes to this process, albeit within the context of solo performance, when he writes that 'expressive techniques are passed from one musician to another by demonstration' (1985: 88). From my experience within ensembles, these actions take place within performance without requiring conversation. However, these applications of transactional leadership elements are not as they would be in a business environment. The achievement/reward system does not exist while playing unless one considers the achievement of a specific 'successful' performance as its own reward. Thus, whilst elements of transactional leadership can be found in ensembles, there is no direct correlation between this form of leadership as found in business and musical performance.

Applying transformational leadership to ensemble contexts presents a unique set of difficulties as associated traits are less task-specific than those of transactional leadership. For example, 'idealised influence' is exerted through a leader acting as a role model, in both a performative and moral sense. In this way, musicians may lead through their own practice and dedication to their craft. 'Inspirational motivation', on the other hand, deals more with long term goal setting. Whilst this may occur amongst ensembles outside of performance, it may not be as evident within. Although it is common to refer to a musician's playing as inspirational, this pertains more to the ethos and ideology of performance itself than embodying specific characteristics. Consequently, attributes of inspirational performance are highly idiosyncratic. More important than understanding the qualities that encompass inspirational performance, however, is recognizing that finding inspiration in others' performances may encourage musicians to develop their own level of playing. This does not mean that 'inspirational' musicians concentrate on exuding that trait: rather, it may be a result of their musical skill. Several other qualities associated with transformational leaders do not apply as easily. Propositional 'intellectual stimulation' is tenuous when related to musical performance, and although the associated use of 'questioning assumptions' and 'reframing problems' is common during conversation, it is difficult to conceive of an equivalent in performance. Likewise, although 'individualised consideration' may occur within ensemble performance, 'the acceptance of individual differences concerning varying needs of autonomy, encouragement, responsibility, or even structure and instructions' holds more in common with pedagogical interaction than peer interaction. Within ensembles, the 'individualised consideration' that occurs is directed towards each musician's sound. Overall, although some musicians may be inspirational to their peers, other aspects of transformational leadership do not appear to exist in non-pedagogical performance.

The application of sociological models of leadership to ensembles calls attention to an aspect of musical interaction not explicitly focused upon in current musicological literature. Recalling Seddon's description of nonverbal communication as including 'body language, facial expression, eye contact, musical cues and gesticulations' (2005: 54), it is curious to note that only one activity mentioned is non-visual. Similarly, Tovstiga et al. remark that communication within a string quartet is primarily nonverbal, occurring 'through collective, inner sensing within the quartet, and through musical-acoustical or visible cues' (2004: 9). That being said, the authors do not elaborate on the nature of 'musical-acoustical' cues. Williamon and Davidson fall into a similar web of assumptions when they comment – without clarification – on the 'acoustical information exchange' that occurs within ensemble performance (2002: 59). Clarke notes this oversight, writing that 'despite the obvious importance of listening and an awareness of each other's breathing, bodily movement, facial gesture etc. as channels of communication, the role of auditory and visual feedback in this whole process remains almost completely uninvestigated' (2002: 61). Whilst visual feedback has been addressed (if only partially) within the past ten years, it is surprising that more research has not explicitly considered aural interaction in performance, given the distinctly auditory nature of music. Hypothetically, it could be presumed that a correspondingly large amount of qualitative information about the music being performed is communicated aurally – an assumption supported by Tovstiga, Williamon and Davidson. However, there has been no further examination of the nature of this information. As the primary output of a musical performance is sound, any additional acoustic information would have to be subtle enough to not distract from the music itself. If performers add extra-musical sounds to the soundscape of the piece (that presumably were not intended by the composer), the performance may not be considered to be of high quality. Granted, live performance is filled with 'nonmusical' sounds that audiences are trained to accept (and, to a certain extent, ignore), including the incidental sounds of instrumental operation such as the click of keys, the sound of breathing and so on.[23]

Although this brief discussion has focused on the 'nonmusical' sounds within musical performance, it is important to remember the amount of exposure musicians have to musical sound itself. Whilst certainly a much larger topic than may be considered in this book, the extent of professional musicians' aural acuity should not be disregarded. That musicians acquire sophisticated means of listening is not a new proposition (Pecenka and Keller, 2009: 285), just as the concept that increased familiarity with a subject increases the amount of discrimination possible is not uncommon outside music. In addition, aural input received by musicians does not occur in isolation; sounds generated through performance are accompanied by other sensory input. When playing in an ensemble, the music created by my coperformers is inextricably linked to their actions and cannot happen without impetus. Therefore, the relationship between sound-producing gestures and the resulting musical output may prove to be vitally important to the dissemination of musical information within an ensemble. Before fully substantiating that claim,

---

[23]   In both vocal and wind instrument performance, the breath preceding note generation is recognized to be pedagogically important (Gaunt, 2007; Kaastra, 2008; Snell, 1997). As a brass player, I have been trained to both listen for and give a preparatory rhythmic breath before I play. To paraphrase countless brass instructors' recommendations to student ensembles, 'if you breathe together, you will play together'. That being said, this breath is not intended to be heard by the audience.

however, it is necessary to examine the relationship of sound-producing gestures to the music being played – the subject of Chapter 4.

Through these discussions, we are left with several large questions. The original thesis question – how do musicians interact and share information with each other while performing? – remains unanswered. Whilst current literature in sociology and musicology addresses some ways in which musicians interact, there has been little progress understanding how information may be shared through performance. Before turning our attention to this issue, however, it is useful to consider what conclusions may be deduced thus far. First, neither linguistic nor gestural models of communication adequately address relationships between ensemble musicians. Likewise, they do not consider (or question) the specific kinds of qualitative musical content that needs to be shared in such relationships. Second, leadership found within small ensembles is highly circumstantial and emerges through any number of developmental contexts. Third, whilst existing leadership models may appear to outwardly correspond to ensemble interaction, we do not know *how* leadership actually operates in musical groups. I propose that this is primarily due to our inability to describe the nature of the information being transferred between coperformers. Beyond these conclusions, however, many further questions arise, falling into two main categories. First, what qualifies as communication within ensemble performance? Does explicit communication (similar to that which exists linguistically) exist? Given 'leadership by example', how are the performance parameters such as tempo, volume and style received and interpreted by their coperformers? Second, how do performers shift between leading and following? Are such shifts intentional? How can musicians achieve fluidity of ensemble role without verbal interaction? These questions prompt a closer investigation of performance, particularly the ways in which musicians may send or receive information (if that is the appropriate description for this activity) and the nature of that information itself. By understanding this process, we will be able to approach how musical information may affect performers' activity within ensembles.

Problematizing Communication

Although some progress has been made in determining how ensembles may share and coordinate qualitative musical information, such research has been unable to do more than identify the nonverbal elements that factor into ensemble interaction. As a result, this identification process has not been able to be condensed into a framework by which interaction itself may be understood. I propose that in this situation musicologists have not been asking the critical questions needed to unpick this aspect of musical performance. This, in turn, may be a result of focusing on propositional Mode 1 knowledge rather than procedural Mode 2 knowledge. As we have seen throughout this chapter, implicit within musicological research on ensembles is a reliance on the paradigm of communication, drawing upon both its process of encoding, transmitting and decoding information, and its associated linguistic terms. Gilboa and Tal-Shmotkin go as far as to describe performance as requiring an 'implicit communication strategy' (2012: 34). With continual references to 'nonverbal communication' (King and Ginsborg, 2011), 'communicative gestures' (Dahl et al., 2010), 'modes of communication' (Seddon and Biasutti, 2009), 'visual communication' (Kokotsaki, 2007) and 'musical communication' (Wilson and MacDonald, 2012), among others, this body of research perpetuates the tacit assumption that performers operate in a manner similar to those involved in conversation. This process, known as the transmission model of communication (c.f. Wilson and MacDonald, 2012), is analogous to that of a telephone or postal service (Garnett, 2010), in which information is packaged into a medium, transmitted to an audience and unpackaged from that medium by the audience. In other words, information is 'pushed' from one person to another through intentional action on behalf of the sender. However, within a musicological context, this paradigm encourages a framework of understanding that is rooted not in musical performance but in social interaction. As a result, reliance upon a paradigm of communication may predispose researchers towards one particular frame of thought, preventing them from engaging with the underlying critical questions at hand. It is therefore necessary to further explore the assumptions propagated by application of this paradigm to musical contexts.

Case Study: The Boult Quartet in Rehearsal

In order to critique the paradigm of communication as a grounding for ensemble interaction, it is useful to begin by considering its direct application to a real world situation.[24] Observation of a professional level ensemble in action provides a context against which this paradigm may be tested. Rather than utilizing a sociological manner of observation – one that would generate Mode 1 knowledge – I approach this case study from the perspective of a fellow musician, drawing upon the Mode 2 knowledge I have accumulated through similar experiences. This may prove to be a useful vantage point in addressing the fundamental question of whether or not communication (as understood in a linguistic manner) actually occurs. The following two videos, taken from a rehearsal by Birmingham Conservatoire's Boult Quartet, present the first and second play-throughs of a short excerpt from the second movement of Samuel Barber's *String Quartet No. 1, Op. 11* (see Example 2.1 for the corresponding excerpt from the score).

---

[24]   Material from this discussion has developed from presentations I have given at the Royal Musical Association Postgraduate Students' Conference at the University of Manchester (January 2011), the Performa'11 Conference on Performance Studies at the University of Aveiro, Portugal (May 2011) and the Centre for Musical Performance as Creative Practice Performance Studies Network International Conference at the University of Cambridge (July 2011).

Example 2.1 Samuel Barber, *String Quartet No. 1, Op. 11.* Movement II, bars 35–40

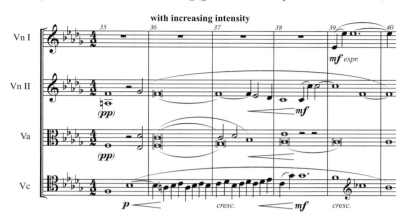

This excerpt contains a single, small musical idea that is picked up by three of the four instruments over two bars. The peak of the cello melody in the fourth bar is emphasized and expanded upon by the second and first violins. In Video Example 2.2, we see the first rehearsal of this excerpt, in which the cellist plays his melody subtly, without a distinct *crescendo* until bar 37.[25] There, he dramatically increases both intensity and volume. Accordingly, his smooth and even bowings in the first three bars give way to larger bow strokes at the peak of his melody. The second violinist and violist play their supporting material at an equal volume, with the violinist's moving line at the end of bar 37 gradually emerging. His subsequent rising octave continues the cellist's line until the first violinist propels the melody even higher. The violist's performance remains aurally and visually unassuming, contrasting the larger motions used by the two violinists on their ascending octaves. In this play-through, the cellist clearly emphasizes the growth of his line from *p* to *mf* and both violinists similarly 'lean into' their rising crotchet lines. Observing the way the musicians are interacting, it is apparent that the quartet members recognize that the cellist has the main line and perform accordingly.

A strict *prima facie* assumption of a communicative paradigm in this situation prompts the following analysis. The cellist has a distinct musical intention – a swell at the peak of his melody – which he wishes to communicate to the rest

---

[25]   Throughout several of the Boult Quartet's rehearsals, the musicians practised with the assistance of a metronome. Clarifying its specific function, the musicians report that playing with the metronome at early stages of rehearsal allows them to focus more on intonation (particularly in keys that are not idiomatic for stringed instruments, as is found in Barber's *String Quartet No. 1*) and coordination while playing at slow tempi. Effectively, the metronome shoulders some of the cognitive burden from the performers, enabling them to concentrate on other musical elements. From my experience, this practice is a commonly used rehearsal technique.

of the quartet. He encodes this musical phrase into aural and visual media, resulting in the sound of his cello and the visible motions of his body. Through playing his instrument, the cellist 'broadcasts' this intention to his coperformers, effectively leading by example. Subsequently, the other quartet members receive this multimodal sensory information, decode it and apply the interpretation to their own performances. In this context, the paradigm does not present any immediate problems and may be tentatively considered valid. However, observation of a single, 'ideal' situation may not reveal significant detail about the underlying processes at play.

What happens should the cellist play in a different manner, as occurs the second time this excerpt is rehearsed? In Video Example 2.3, the cellist begins this play-through in a similar manner to the previous, but is noticeably caught in the middle of an awkward bowing at the end of bar 37. This prevents him from executing the indicated *crescendo* to the extent that he did previously, resulting in a markedly softer rendition of the rising two-note motif. The second violinist distinctly watches the cellist in bars 37 and 38, witnessing the smaller (if accidental) gestures used. Accordingly, the second violinist adjusts the way that he executes his ascending octave line, playing the figure softer and more unassuming than in the previous take. The first violinist, however, does not alter his playing as much as the second.

In comparison to the first video example, communicative analysis of the second play-through results in a different conclusion. The second play-through highlights an aspect of human activity not explicitly found in the first: unintentionality. The cellist did not necessarily intend to underestimate the amount of bow available for him to use at the peak of his melody. Nevertheless, the fact that he did so provided aural and visual information to the rest of the quartet. Upon receiving this information, they adjusted their performances accordingly. Re-examining the paradigm of communication within these circumstances, the stages of transmission and decoding remain intact and function as they have previously. The encoding stage, however, is either incorrectly executed or generates incorrect data – a musical concept that the cellist does not intend to transmit.[26] In light of this, we are left with the following question: is the expression of qualitative information, the process previously described in terms of communication, limited to communicative gestures? How may musicians acquire information about their coperformers' interpretations and performances while they are currently happening? A more fruitful avenue of inquiry than has been undertaken thus far in this chapter, therefore, is to consider how the other musicians inferred information from the cellist's actions regardless of whether they were intentional. Intention

---

[26] It is worth noting that this situation is not unique within ensemble rehearsal. Idiosyncrasy and spontaneity are commonly encouraged within performance of Western art music. Unexpected changes to performance context (such as a change in another musician's individual performance) may prove to be the catalyst for creative alteration of musical interpretation. For further discussion of the role performers' individuality may play in the creation of a performance, see Kivy, 1995: 128.

complicates the communicative paradigm that the models of communication and leadership are implicitly based upon, as both explicit communication and leadership are, by nature, intentional.[27] Alexander Jensenius et al. question whether or not an action has to be 'carried out consciously in order to be perceived as a gesture', allowing for 'ambiguous cases where one person may perceive an action as intentional and another person may see it as unintentional' (2010: 18). Thus, the attribution of intention plays a primary role in communication. Literary theorist Stanley Fish remarks that 'words are intelligible only within the assumption of some context of intentional production, some already-in-place predecision as to what kind of person, with what kind of purposes, in relation to what specific goals in a particular situation is speaking or writing' (1989: 295, emphasis removed). This statement may apply aptly to the interpretation of communicative gestures. Thus, we are left with a framework in which explicit communication is understood at the abandonment of other avenues by which information may be transferred. Questions about how musicians share information within performance (hence, addressing Mode 2 knowledge) cannot be addressed simply by categorizing the gestures being used, as that propositional form of taxonomy will generate copious amounts of data without an underlying rationale. To fully unravel the process by which musical interpretations are shared amongst ensemble performers, we must turn our attention away from musical groups and focus on the phenomenon of musical performance. It is only through an understanding of performance from the perspective of Mode 2 knowledge that we may adequately address ensemble interaction.

The Problem of Intention

As the previous example demonstrates, intentionality may significantly alter what originally appears to be a straightforward paradigm of communication. Recognizing the enormous complexity surrounding notions of intention and action, this book must be limited to only the most pertinent associated theories. When discussing intention, it is vital to distinguish between intention from the perspective of the person acting and that which is attributed to the actor by an observer, forms of intention described by Maurice Merleau-Ponty as 'intentionality of act' and 'operative intentionality' (1945: xx). Bearing this distinction in mind, Chapter 4 investigates intentionality of act in relation to the phenomenology of an individual performer, isolating the processes within personal intention. In order to determine the correlation (if any) between a performer's internal musical ideas and their subsequent performance, it is necessary to determine the extent to which their actions are intentionally conducted. After establishing a framework for

---

[27] Whilst it is possible to unintentionally communicate something, the concept has more to do with the breakdown of the communicative paradigm than unintentional expression. As illustrated by the colloquial phrase 'sending the wrong signals', the act of 'sending' may be intentional, but the outcome is not.

understanding intentionality of an action within musical performance in Chapter 4, it will be possible to explore operative intentionality (intention that is attributed upon one's actions by an observer) in Chapter 5. Reconsidering the rehearsal example above, the quartet members may or may not have attributed intention to the cellist's actions. Within this ostensibly minor rehearsal event, the musicians are forced to actively gauge not only whether or not their coperformers' actions are intended or accidental, but also how to suitably react.

Whilst a brief overview of current philosophic research on intention is imperative in order to consider the relationship of mental concepts (or perceived mental concepts) to subsequent actions, there remains an essential unanswered question as to the nature of the information being actively shared by ensemble musicians. The next chapter will explore characteristics of this information, allowing us to construct a clearer picture of the knowledge that may impact on performance. Through an understanding of the musical content being expressed (and the entailments acoustic information may yield), we may then examine the role intention may play within ensembles.

Chapter 3
A Question of Content

In the previous chapter, I have demonstrated how current models of communication and the paradigm of communication itself are unsatisfactory in describing how musicians interact and share information. The processes by which variables such as tempo, dynamics, intonation, phrasing and interpretation are coordinated during performance are not found in other social interactions. What has become equally apparent is that the information being shared by musicians falls firmly within the realm of Mode 2 knowledge. Whilst it may be possible to describe characteristics of this information in a propositional manner (for example, specific metronome markings and pitches), other linguistic or visual descriptions may merely allude to a musical interpretation. Therefore, it is necessary to examine the nature of this information, including how musicians engage with it both during and outside performance. This chapter attempts to identify the nature of musical information and, correspondingly, musical thought. From this starting point, it may be possible to develop a more thorough understanding of the phenomenology of musical performance: the underlying structure required to approach the question of how musicians interact.

The content of a musical performance may engender different kinds of information dependent upon the perceiver. Leonard Meyer puts this most succinctly when he writes that 'whether a piece of music gives rise to affective experience or to intellectual experience depends upon the disposition and training of the listener' (1994: 34). Whilst I do not believe that affective experience is necessarily opposite to intellectual experience, these terms may usefully distinguish between what may be generalized as the audiences' and performers' experience. Rather than interpreting the content of a musical performance through an emotional or affective lens, performers may interpret the same content in a much more technical manner. Lutz Jäncke calls this process extraction, writing that 'musicians, relative to non-musicians, pre-attentively extract more information from musically relevant stimuli' (2006: 34). It is not a matter of musicians hearing different musical content, but hearing musical content differently.

How then may we understand the ways in which musicians perceive musical content? The most direct source would be the musical content itself. However, this presents multiple issues. Should I hypothetically unravel every entailment arising from a simple musical phrase, I would only be listing possible interpretations. The task would be as monumental (and as unproductive) as trying to list every entailment of the colour blue. Likewise, the list of possibilities that I would arrive at is limited to that which emerges from my personal experience and background. As Rita Aiello writes, 'although the meaning of music is enhanced by our knowledge of musical styles and practices, musical meaning remains both pluralistic and personal' (1994: 55). Whilst Aiello focuses on the creation and interpretation of musical meaning, the same conclusions may be made when considering the more technical information ensemble members may extract within performance. The information I extract from musical content is not merely informed by my perspective, but regulated by it. My capacity for research is bound by my own subjective experience. Thus, a personal account of musical content may be considered both boundless and restricted: boundless in that there is no apparent upper limit to the possible entailments of musical content and restricted in that the entailments categorized by an individual are regulated by his or her perspective and background.

Given this dichotomy, how else may the question of musical content be addressed? Although musical experience is subjective, performers regularly function efficiently and cohesively within ensembles. The most direct way of observing musicians relate concepts about music to each other would be to watch rehearsal and performance. However, this does not resolve the matter of the researcher's subjective experience and perception. Aside from performance, I would argue that the next most direct way musicians engage with musical content is to talk about it with one another. Whilst musical experience is certainly personal, there must be enough similarity (or socially agreed similarity) between individuals' experiences that language may act as a mediating tool. Thus, performers' language when discussing musical content may provide a useful window into their personal experience of that content.

This chapter is broken up into three primary sections. The first section explores how musical information is interpreted and shared through metaphor. Ostensibly nonmusical terminology serves as one method by which performers may describe musical content and experiences efficiently and effectively. However, it will become clear that metaphors are not limited to purely linguistic descriptions of musical content. The second section expands the concept of metaphor to include other modes of experience, particularly physical motion and visual abstraction. This leads to an examination of music not merely as an aural event but as a mode of experience in upon itself. Out of these discussions, the third section of this chapter describes the characteristics of musical information as interpreted by performing musicians. From this perspective, it is possible to fully examine more closely the mechanisms of ensemble performance.

Musical Language, Musical Thought

Rehearsal discussions draw on technical terminology that is often specific to the realm of music. Although the words themselves may be frequently used in other fields, they may be imbued with an entirely different set of connotative implications within a musical context. In this section, I will investigate how musicians use this language during rehearsal. Those familiar with rehearsal practice should not find the examples being used as extraordinary; I deliberately chose to highlight common turns of phrase. The phrases themselves are not important to the argument presented through this book, however. Instead, their importance lies in the fundamental relationship between these phrases and the musical content they describe. An understanding of this relationship may provide insight into how musicians conceive of music itself, bringing us one step closer to unravelling the enigma of Mode 2 musical knowledge.

Terminology utilized within rehearsal may not originally appear to be as technical as may be found in other fields as it draws upon common words and phrases. These 'borrowed' words – those not originally used within musical discourse – serve primarily as descriptors, creating a host of connotative associations through which certain concepts may be more succinctly understood. Through the application of 'nonmusical' terminology, musical elements may be expressed in a linguistically economical manner. John Dewey explains that language does not need to correlate directly with a concept, particularly when considering art as a quality of experience rather than an object:

> Not only is it impossible that language should duplicate the infinite variety of individualized qualities that exist, but it is wholly undesirable and unneeded that it should do so. The unique quality of a quality is found in experience itself; it is there and sufficiently there not to need reduplication in language. (1934: 224)

Thus, language – specifically, metaphoric language – provides the practical means by which people may refer to experience. George Lakoff and Mark Johnson, in their seminal work *Metaphors We Live By*, describe the essence of metaphor as 'understanding and experiencing one kind of thing in terms of another' (1980: 5). They argue that humans conceive of the world through a web of interrelationships by which many disparate concepts are understood. The resulting language, whilst economical, retains a richness of meaning and depth.

For example, timbre is often described within musical discourse using terminology normally associated with physical texture. In a rehearsal of the Boult Quartet, the violist comments that the use of a certain hand position on the neck of her instrument will result in a note that is 'not going to be very strong … It's going to sound fluffy because it's right at the top of the C [string]' (Rehearsal 2, 09:52). Although the term 'fluffy' is not technical, it does encourage a mental association between the way that note will sound and a soft material's texture. Furthermore, the soft material associated with the sound with may have other physical properties that may be beneficially extrapolated: for example, absence of definite edges or a solid core. The extension of metaphorical relationships between two concepts is identified by Lakoff and Johnson as a metaphorical entailment: 'a coherent system of metaphorical concepts [combined with] a corresponding coherent system of metaphorical expressions for those concepts' (1980: 9). Consequently, it is not uncommon for tone quality to be described as 'rough', 'bright', 'warm', and so on.

Metaphorical entailments afford a wealth of cognitive associations by which the timbres may be understood.

In addition to comparing timbre to texture, musical lines may be described in relationship to the kinds of movement. Two rehearsal comments directed towards the first violinist of the Boult Quartet highlight this association. At one point, the second violinist points out that the first 'suddenly [goes] to a more static line', a melody that contains less variation in pitch and note duration (Rehearsal 2, 22:36). The musical line itself does not actually move in physical space: rather, it 'moves' between notes. The second violinist can characterize this melody in terms of spatial movement due to the mutually understood entailment between pitch, rhythm and physical motion. The widespread use of this form of metaphor has been noted by Rolf Godøy, who writes that the 'use of spatial concepts can be applied to several other features of musical sound such as intensity (*crescendo*, *decrescendo*) and tempo (*accelerando*, *ritardando*), texture (spread, focused, thick, thin) and so on, or to more general and composite sensations such as [the] increase or decrease of tension' (2010: 113). Later in the Boult Quartet rehearsal, a comment by the cellist creates a stronger cognitive relationship between musical line and motion:

> **Cello**: [First Violin], I think you could be more, especially at [rehearsal marking] two … could be a bit more physical. It needs it, it's muscular music, to be honest. I don't think it's any room for poncing –
> **Viola**: … muscular music … [laughs]
> **Cello**: It is, though, isn't it? It's not pissing about, is it?
>
> (Rehearsal 2, 1:17:05)

The cellist's description of this musical line imbues it with not only a sense of physical motion, but also character. The language used calls to mind associations with determination and decisiveness, almost anthropomorphizing the line. Whilst the violist laughs at the terminology, the metaphor is effective in that it arouses a level of mental imagery that may not be present when describing the musical content in more technical terms (for example, specific volume, frequency and so on).

Beyond the compelling usage of borrowed terminology as qualitative descriptors, the ways in which musicians talk about their relationship to the music itself is revealing. Specific musical units or characteristics are referred to in a variety of ways, particularly in terms of objects, physical qualities or locations. Table 3.1 provides examples of this metaphoric language, all taken from the second filmed rehearsal of the Boult Quartet. The ease of which I found the following examples within a single rehearsal illustrates the frequency with which such language is used.

Musicians' performances themselves may be objectified in a similar manner, and treated as if they were physical locations. For example, a common criticism amongst musicians is that they are playing behind or ahead of the beat. The entailment of musical content as location is further emphasized through the comparison of a musical piece to a landscape, as the violist comments 'Can we … go

Table 3.1   Examples of metaphor in rehearsal language

Referent	Quality	Rehearsal example
Object	Given	'[You] do have to give [that quaver] to us.' [Cello, 1:11:08]
		'I'll give that bar before [rehearsal marking] seven.' [Cello, 13:59]
	Possessed	'At the Più tranquillo, … neither of you have rhythm.' [First Violin, 24:52]
	Lost	'I just don't know how I'm going to find [that pitch].' [Viola, 07:58]
Physical property	Size	'If I make the accent bigger like you were suggesting, it's going to seem … it's going to feel like a downbeat.' [Cello, 36:44]
	Length	'I feel the rest is too short, to me. It feels too short.' [Second Violin, 40:00]
Location		'Where do you come in after the key change?' [Cello, 41:05]
		'We're not coming off the minims together.' [First Violin, 38:18]
		'It feels as though … these guys are slightly behind me.' [Cello, 1:07:36]

from [rehearsal marking] eleven, but slowly to the end … so I can kind of get the geography of it all' (Rehearsal 2, 28:02).

   Examination of metaphoric language in use allows us to not only understand how musicians verbally agree upon variables in ensemble performance, but also to glimpse how musicians engage with musical interpretation. As Lakoff and Johnson write that humans grasp concepts as 'fundamentally metaphorical in nature', language is a powerful tool when investigating human conceptual systems (1980: 3). The rehearsal language used by performers may indicate both how they adapt nontechnical terminology to represent musical concepts and how they mentally perceive those concepts in the first place. Recalling Lakoff and Johnson's definition of metaphor as 'understanding and experiencing one kind of thing in terms of another' (Ibid.: 5), metaphor is not only linguistic in nature, but also phenomenological. In later research, the authors propose that humans' experience interacting with the physical world creates a form of phenomenological embodiment, the underpinnings by which our minds may create metaphors (1999: 36). The body, they write, 'is not merely somehow involved in conceptualization but is shaping its very nature' (Ibid.: 37). Along these lines, musicians create and use metaphoric language that correlates what may be ostensibly complex musical content with physical experience. Likewise, these metaphors enable humans (looking beyond musician/nonmusician categories) to represent musical concepts internally. In discussing timbre, Tor Halmrast et al. point out that 'the widespread use of metaphors such as "grainy," "smooth," "rough," … etc. among both experts and novices is a testimony to the existence of more or less distinct concepts of timbral features in the minds of listeners' (2010: 184). Therefore, the term 'fluffy' does not just serve as the placeholder for a timbre, but it begets the mental imagery by which that timbre is understood.

Terminology such as 'mental imagery' is not unfamiliar to practising musicians. To what may this imagery specifically refer? Mental imagery may not only include internal representations of musical variables (timbre, volume, style, and so on), but also representations of specific characteristics of ensemble performance itself (cohesive entrances and exits, active adjustment of intonation and the like). Internal mental representations of musical content are grounded both in experience and imagination. The language used by performers arises from attempts to verbally represent musical elements through comparison to other forms of experience. Correspondingly, there is a complex taxonomy of metaphorical categories that may be recognized in rehearsal language. Applying nonmusical metaphorical categories proposed by Lakoff and Johnson, there may exist:

- orientational metaphors ('I'm in the *lower* register of an instrument' or 'Our semiquavers are getting *behind*');
- ontological metaphors ('Can we play the *soft* section again?' or 'We need a much *warmer* sound');
- action metaphors ('Who has the *moving* line?' or 'It's right after your *flurry* of notes'); and
- metaphors built on complex relationships ('His sound is very *rich*' or 'You're playing very *aggressively* there').[1]

This taxonomy is not codified by any means, as musicians continuously forge new relationships between musical elements and language. It is not uncommon for ensembles to arrive at their own vocabulary derived from their collective experiences playing together. The associations made between experience and specific musical elements encourage organic development of language in a manner that may not be easily categorized. However, lack of codification does not detract from the efficacy of this language. As mentioned before, the use of new or unexpected language ('muscular music', for example) may evoke vivid mental imagery. Such language engages with imagination in such a way as to expose one's interpretation of elements within musical content, thus providing a unique source of insight that may be present (but technically indescribable) in performance.

---

[1] For an examination of these categories in relation to musical analysis, see Saslaw, 1996.

The Multimodality of Musical Phenomena

Just as idiosyncratic language reveals elements of musicians' underlying thought processes and interpretation, so too the contexts within which the language is used provide insight. Lakoff and Johnson's definition of metaphor as 'understanding and experiencing one kind of thing in terms of another' does not specify that either the subject or the referent has to be linguistic, a point they raise in subsequent research (1999: 57). Consequently, musical content may not only be understood through the linguistic metaphor of physical motion, but also through physical motion itself. Consider the following excerpt from a rehearsal by the Boult Quartet.[2] During a break from the second movement of Samuel Barber's *String Quartet No. 1*, the cellist remarks 'You know, it is worth, in the future, practising [bars 52–53]. 'Cos, actually, that's one of those things that, in a concert, is going to be a lot harder' (Video Example 3.1, 00:17; see Example 3.1 for the corresponding excerpt from the score).

Example 3.1 Samuel Barber, *String Quartet No. 1, Op. 11*. Movement II, bars 52–53

The two bars the cellist describes arguably contain the most dynamic contrast in the entire work. At the conclusion of a prolonged ascent, the quartet plays an extremely loud, sustained chord, followed by a hushed *pianissimo* chorale. On paper, it appears as if the primary contrast is of dynamics. However, the way the cellist characterizes this excerpt to his peers highlights the nuances of his interpretation. Rather than describing the perceived contrast using technical terminology or by physically playing his instrument, the cellist both vocalizes

---

[2]   Material from this discussion developed from a presentation I gave at the Royal Musical Association Postgraduate Students' Conference at the University of Manchester (January 2011).

and dramatically gesticulates his interpretation. These different forms of representation provide insight into his musical intention for these bars, as well as highlight other contrasts not explicit in the score. From an aural standpoint, the cellist's vocalization illuminates two areas of contrast in his interpretation. The first concerns dynamics: whilst the first note the cellist sings is not very loud – especially in relationship to the volume of his spoken voice – the second note is inaudible. Although no sound is produced at this entrance, the cellist's motions inform observers that the note still exists. The second contrast is that of timbre. To say that the cellist sings the first note is to use the verb loosely: the timbre is very raspy and harsh, more like an exhalation than musical vocalization. This attributes a brutal and raw character to that note, particularly in sharp contrast to the subdued nature of the following section. These contrasts are corroborated through the cellist's physical motions. While vocalizing the first note, he uses his right arm to mime moving the bow across his instrument in a large and controlled manner. Upon completion of that note, however, he then shifts from a playing motion to a much more subtle conducting motion, indicating the placement of the second note.

The way the cellist describes his interpretation of these two notes highlights an important characteristic of the constituent aspects of musical phenomena. Through his representation of this excerpt, the cellist illustrates how, for him, sound and spatial movement are integrally related to musical content. Rather than translate his interpretation into language, he simultaneously expresses one 'domain of experience' in terms of two others. Rolf Godøy writes that:

> The constant shift between perceiving and acting, or between listening and making (or only imagining) gestures, means that music perception is embodied in the sense that it is closely linked with bodily experience … and that music perception is multimodal in the sense that we perceive music with the help of both visual/kinematic images and effort/dynamics sensations, in addition to the 'pure' sound. (2010: 105)

By expressing his interpretative intention (or, alternatively, his mental image) of this excerpt in aural and spatial forms without his instrument, the cellist demonstrates the multimodality of musical phenomena.

Rehearsals are filled with multimodal exchanges similar to the one just analysed. Musicians may use many alternatives in how they refer to a specific musical excerpt, ranging from purely technical (as if describing written notation) to the purely instrumental. These forms of reference may act as placeholders for specific musical excerpts, facilitating conversation. At the verbal end of the spectrum, a musician may dictate specific score locations, notes and rhythms using explicit terminology. Performers may alternatively use pronouns to refer to expressive markings or other descriptors in place of a specific bar number. These pronouns may give way to simple descriptions of the musical phrase in question: the most generic linguistic means of referring to a musical excerpt. Beyond these verbal descriptions, simple vocalized passages may serve as placeholders. The accuracy of these vocalizations is typically not highly prioritized, as they act as caricatures rather than strict recreations. As long as their representative function is fulfilled, their resemblance to the original musical material is irrelevant. Finally, the need for placeholders may be obviated through instrumental performance of the excerpt itself (as it would appear in performance or abbreviated). These categories are neither well defined nor strictly used independent of each other. Placeholders may be used interchangeably, alternating between categories. For example, a verbal description of an excerpt may be followed by an instrumental abbreviation for clarification. Alternatively, a quick play-through of an excerpt may require further clarification of the score, which may be better suited to technical explanation. Rehearsals teem with these multimodal exchanges, transcribed examples of which may be found in Table 3.2. Due to the mixed mediums within which these exchanges exist, linguistic transcription does not fully convey the manner in which they operate. Therefore, examples of multimodal comments taken from rehearsals of the Boult Quartet may be found on the DVD that accompanies this book. The times indicated after each comment refer to their starting point within Video Example 3.2. Within examples of integrated conversation, indicated times refer to the beginning of the conversations themselves.

The interchangeable nature of technical terminology, general descriptions, vocalizations and instrumental performance suggests that these exchanges are rooted in how musical content is mentally conceived rather than acting purely as placeholders for musical content. Metaphor can only exist through the utilization of historical personal experience of the original musical content and the external concept to which it is being compared. As Lakoff and Johnson write, 'no metaphor can ever be comprehended or even adequately represented independently of its experiential basis' (1980: 19). Therefore, in order for placeholders to function within rehearsal language, performers need to have concrete experience both with musical elements and the physical world with which it correlates. For example, if a musician were to describe a timbre as brittle, yet none of their peers knew what brittle meant (or had no practical experience with anything brittle), the metaphor would be incompatible with the experiences shared by the performers. Regardless of how perfectly 'brittle' described the original timbre, the word would not allow the other musicians to construct similar timbres in their minds. Similarly, even if someone may imagine what sonic qualities a brittle timbre might have, they would be unable to imagine that timbre applied to an instrument they had never heard before. As metaphors allow us 'to understand one domain of experience in terms of another', music may be consequently conceived as a domain of experience in itself. However, this proposition raises the question of how to identify such musical experience. If performers relate experience in the physical world to experience in music, by extension the 'musical world' must be able to be understood not only in metaphorical terms, but in terms of the music itself. It cannot have a partial existence, only conceivable through metaphor. To draw on an overused idiom, regardless of whether a picture is worth a thousand words, that picture does not

Table 3.2   The spectrum of musical referents

Mode of representation	Rehearsal example
Linguistic (explicit)	'The last quaver of the five/four bar is an upbow.' [First Violin, 00:12] 'I go from a G♮ to a G♯.' [Cello, 00:27]
Linguistic (referential)	'Let's just go from there, on the nose, yeah? That high sustained note.' [Cello, 00:43] 'Perhaps, don't do it over the four/four bar and the next three/four bar, don't do any stringendo there while we're coming in together, getting off our long B and your little motif; and then you get one bar to get us together and then we can start speeding up again for the last four bars …' [First Violin, 00:57]
Vocalized	'Let's just do those, both those [da da da dee, da dee dee dee] passages 'cause they're both dog.' [Cello, 01:27] 'No, I think it's not that slow; I don't think it's that slow … [starts singing] … you go like this.' [Second Violin, 01:49] 'I think if it's the last time they play [dye yupdum], just count 'one two three [ba ba baa]'… that's what I think.' [First Violin, 02:15]
Performed	'I'll give you [three bar excerpt], 'K? … I'll give that bar before seven.' [Cello, 02:34] 'Do you like that upbow? [three-note figure] Is that what you went for? [First Violin, 02:46] 'For some reason we got an accent on [three-note figure] … and it wasn't a small accent.' [Viola, 02:53]
Integrated	'That's likely to be an upbow, I don't mind. [three-note figure] 'Cos then you have a long –' [First Violin, 03:05] '– On the [dee da dah]? OK, yeah?' [Cello] 'Do we have to? Because then I have to start on [two bar excerpt of viola line] …' [Viola] 'What's wrong with that? [three-note figure]' [Cello, 03:23] 'You can't get the separation.' [Viola] 'What, what separation?' [Cello] '[Da da dah]' [Viola] 'Is that [three-note figure]?' [Cello] 'It needs another bowing –' [First Violin] '– To me you can hear [da dit dah]: [three-note figure] – ' [Cello] '– But not as clearly as if you hear [three-note figure], so if you do two bows …' [First Violin] 'No, it's two [bows].' [Second Violin] 'Why don't we do [two-bar excerpt of violin line, with repetition of last phrase]?' [Second Violin, 03:52] 'To finish up on a –' [First Violin] '– To do the fortissimo on an upbow. [miniature version of excerpt]' [Second Violin] 'You'll still have the same problem with your longer C, then, do you?' [First Violin] 'Yeah, but still … [last part of excerpt, repeated] [Second Violin]

need to be verbalized in order to be understood: it can be grasped purely through visual terms. Similarly, music does not need to be verbalized in order to be comprehended. That being said, the premise of a musical 'domain of experience' begets a host of entailments, including the proposition that music may serve not only as a mode of interaction but also as a form of knowledge.

This proposition extends the discussion of the modes of knowledge begun in Chapter 1. The existence of terminology specific to musical performance creates issues in dissemination comparable to that found in other specialized fields. Donald Schön describes the difficulties of sharing this form of Mode 2 knowledge:

> Because of the importance of this feel for media and language, an experienced practitioner cannot convey the art of his practice to a novice merely by describing his procedures, rules, and theories, nor can he enable a novice to think like a seasoned practitioner merely by describing or even demonstrating his ways of thinking. Because of the differences in feel for media, language, and repertoire, the art of one practice tends to be opaque to the practitioners of another. (1983: 271)

Thus, the opacity of rehearsal vocabulary results from the 'feel' that musicians have for the 'media and languages of their practices'. As mentioned previously, rehearsal vocabulary evolves in an organic manner, based upon the individual experiences of musicians rather than a collective codification. Although this may appear to present difficulties when musicians interact together, it is important to recall that the language used in rehearsal complements the music itself. In discussion, performers look for metaphors to describe what is *already understood* as musical content. Musical experience (both as a performer and a listener) is vital to creating and interpreting rehearsal language.

The resistance musical elements give to 'translation' into other modes of discourse may also be seen in the notational gap that arises when attempting to graphically notate sonic events. As notation provides the means by which musicians may share instructions on the creation of sonic events, reading notation requires a depth of musical experience in order to correlate images with specific musical elements. Notation cannot recreate all of the information required to produce musical content, creating a 'generative environment' that requires 'iterative interpretation' (Rebelo, 2010: 25). The ambiguity inherent in notation becomes increasingly prominent as scores eschew traditional symbols in favour of 'graphic notation' (a term that begs the question as to what 'non-graphic' notation might be). To a certain extent, the perceptual issues that arise when performing graphic scores has always existed with musical notation; the key difference is the degree to which the abstract symbols have been codified within Western art music. Writing about the nuanced (and often over-simplified) relationship between graphic scores and modern art, Sylvia and Stuart Smith remark that:

> It is the very abstractness of artwork that gives it meaning. The abstractness makes the artwork inextricably ambiguous. This ambiguity that every artwork has allows

for the process of completion – the filling in of missing or ambiguous aspects – in the mind of the viewer. In this way, individual interpretations and reinterpretations of a work are added to the cultural conventions of notation, according to one's personal idiosyncrasies and one's own history within the culture. (1981: 80)

Although the authors talk directly about art, their comments equally apply to musical notation, regardless of the extent to which codification has occurred. The ambiguity found within notation allows 'for the process of completion' in the mind of the performers who interact with it. They have to 'fill in missing or ambiguous aspects', gradually adding to the body of socially agreed conventions for how notation is interpreted. In order for musical notation to be performed, it needs to be read by someone who understands and shares the same system of visual, spatial and musical entailments. Further parallels between the interpretation of art and the realization of musical notation may be drawn as Smith and Smith continue, writing that 'the less highly defined the artwork, the greater is the variety of completion possibilities and therefore multiple reinterpretations' (Ibid.: 80). The relationship between notational precision and available interpretations is most evident when considering the difference between performances from jazz or rock lead sheets (which generally only contain a melody and chord changes) and a highly descriptive score found in Western art music. Whilst neither can fully reproduce the sonic events that they reference, the lack of definition within a lead sheet gives rise to a larger range of interpretations than would be found within Western art music. Likewise, these interpretations are generally of a much larger magnitude, possibly impacting on instrumentation, arrangement and form. The ability to infer musical meaning from notation (as well as rehearsal language, conducting gestures and other modes of musical representation) is dependent upon corresponding musical experience. In order to understand and effectively use the entailments embedded within non-aural representations of music, a performer needs to have significant experience with both the medium of music and the fields referenced by the metaphor, regardless of the mode used.

Characteristics of Musical Information

Building on the previous discussions, it is possible to compile characteristics of the information shared within ensemble performance. Whilst content of this information is directly tied to the piece being performed (or, rather, the specific performance itself), the nature of such information may be distilled into three characteristics: its multimodality, its basis in experience and its contextual subjectivity.

First, musical information is multimodal. Whilst the majority of this information is aural, elements of it may be metaphorically expressed in other mediums. Verbal descriptions of musical events or characteristics use linguistic metaphors to draw comparisons between musical sound and textural or ontological characteristics, physical orientation, motion or even complex anthropomorphized relationships.

Notation depicts musical events and parameters through a combination of predetermined symbols, visual metaphors and written text. Superficially, the physical movements made by people who are engaging with music – particularly performers, conductors and to a lesser extent dancers and listeners moving sympathetically along with a performance – reinterpret musical information within a spatial context. As the next chapter will illustrate, however, the movements made by performers may emerge through a variety of physiological mechanisms, serving distinct purposes tied to the production of musical sound. All of the modes by which musical information may be expressed, short of performance itself, may only contain certain aspects of musical information. Regardless of how specific and thorough the linguistic description, score or gesture, it cannot fully replicate all of the information contained within musical sound itself. As a result, musical information is often expressed through multiple modes simultaneously. When musicians talk about musical excerpts, they express information to their fellow performers through an amalgamated approach of aural, visual and even spatial means. Nonmusical realms of experience such as language, physical motion and graphical abstractions serve as common denominators in clarifying and communicating musical information amongst multiple people. By extension, the way musicians perform includes aspects of this informational content: the central issue to be explored within the remainder of this book.

Second, the amount and kind of musical information extracted from a performance is dependent upon the perceiver's experience and context. Whilst it is obvious that the more background one has with music the more detailed information they can discern from a performance, the implications of this point directly impact on the way ensemble performance may be understood. Playing music with others requires not only a different mindset from being an audience member but also a different way of listening. Experienced musicians are not necessarily 'hearing more' than novices within a performance; rather, they can extract the musical information most pertinent to their specific circumstances. The information within performances and recordings is so concentrated that even a single note may contain the germ of musical characteristics such as tempo, volume, articulation, style, genre and character. These elements of musical information become increasingly evident to those who have significant experience listening to and creating musical sound.

Third, musical information is defined by its contextual subjectivity. As has been established thus far, musical information may be expressed both through performance and the application of multimodal metaphors. Understanding and creating metaphors to express this information requires significant musical experience. However, the amount and kind of information that is deduced from a performance is highly dependent upon context. A single musical excerpt, played to multiple musicians, is bound to give rise to a variety of entailments. Recalling Aiello's comment that musical meaning is 'both pluralistic and personal' (1994: 55), it may not be necessary to specify or categorize minute elements of musical information in order to grasp its nature. Through metaphor, performers can prioritize and correlate information within ensembles without necessarily constricting the range of possible musical entailments.[3] Thus, musical information is fluid in the sense that it may not only engage multiple senses and realms of experience simultaneously, but it does so in completely different ways dependent upon the background and context of those experiencing the performance.

Through this chapter, it has become increasingly apparent that research into musical performance requires engagement with Mode 2 knowledge. To not acknowledge the fundamental difference between propositional and practical knowledge would result in collections of observations: categories of terminology and processes without an underlying rationale. Through such an approach, vital concerns regarding the creation and dissemination of knowledge would remain inaccessible. There is a fluidity to Mode 2 knowledge that neither depends on classifications nor is limited to categories or formulae. It would be impossible to create an encyclopaedia of this knowledge, as it works through imprecision and idiosyncrasy. As we turn our attention to the phenomenology of musical performance, it is necessary to proceed with the awareness that we are clearly dealing within the realm of Mode 2 knowledge.

Conclusion

At this point in the book, it is worth taking stock in the principal conclusions arrived at thus far. Through the previous chapters, I have found that research that applies sociological models of communication and leadership to ensemble interaction is flawed and incomplete. Whilst there is a wealth of possible models and theories that may be applied to ensembles, a fundamental understanding of the phenomenology of performance is absent. When compared with practical experience (which theoretically should be the litmus test for a field called 'performance studies'), the research available does not sufficiently account for the complexity inherent in musical practice. That being said, the previous discussions afford four primary conclusions that may aid in resolving the research questions posed within this text. Evaluation of these conclusions will provide the basis upon which a new paradigm of understanding ensemble interaction may be established.

First, attempts at categorizing gestures within ensemble performance have neglected to identify how the gestures are used and what those gestures might signify to musicians. The umbrella classification of 'communicative gesture', although commonly used, has not been qualified with regard to what information is being communicated. Additionally, there is a lack of consensus (and, in most cases, critical discussion) over the format this information may take. Research

---

[3]   As a performer, I would argue that dissonance between contextual interpretations of musical content gives rise to creative development within ensemble performance. Should a performance be reducible to a formula or mere sequence of actions, its outcome would risk becoming predictable and stale.

that applies non-musicological theories of interaction to musical performance appears to forget that the context is intrinsically different from linguistic or social conditions. Therefore, it is necessary to investigate the information shared in performance and the means of its exchange.

Second, whilst leadership is a common topic within ensemble research, there is little understanding of how musicians may exert leadership in performance. Similarly, although current research has classified the roles that may be present in ensembles, the processes by which ensemble members assume those roles have not been identified. Bearing this in mind, the way in which leadership operates within ensembles shows similarities to the business management model of alternating leadership. In order to substantiate this claim, however, it is necessary to comprehensively understand the experience of ensemble performance – a phenomenon that I would argue has more in common with solo musical performance than with nonmusical social interaction.

Third, research on ensemble interaction tacitly presumes that musicians require explicit communication in order to share information. This assumption originates from the paradigm of communication that underlies most (if not all) research on coperformer interaction. As I have discussed, the communicative paradigm fails to explain the full range of interaction that occurs within ensembles. This is particularly the case when considering the effects of ostensibly unintentional (or not explicitly intentional) actions during performance. I have shown that it is possible for unintentional actions to create the impression of successful communication; however, this circumstance appears to be an example of inference rather than explicit communication. This rehearsal example used is not unique within ensemble performance and engenders the impulsive, idiosyncratic creativity that is recognized to be aesthetically pleasing in musical performance regardless of the genre. Given the inadequacy of the communicative paradigm to account for more than the 'ideal' contexts of ensemble interaction (if it can truly do so), a different approach is needed.

Fourth, musical phenomena are multimodal experiences that are understood by musicians through a variety of unique and flexible metaphors. Extending Lakoff and Johnson's proposition that metaphors 'allow us to understand one domain of experience in terms of another', I propose that musical thinking may be a mode of thought in itself. Therefore, when musicians participate in ensemble performance, they actively draw upon a specific form of musical Mode 2 knowledge. Recognizing the formidable philosophical and epistemological implications of this claim, validation of this proposal requires further reflective practice upon the phenomenology of musical performance in solo and ensemble contexts.

These conclusions and their proposed solutions clearly require critical review. The first step towards clarification of the ways musicians engage with musical concepts within performance is to examine the phenomenology of individual performance itself. Consequently, the next chapter will explore the third research question of this book: given that the performer affects the music being played, to what extent does the inverse apply? The interaction between musician and instrument is a fundamental element of performance, yet has received little critical review outside of pedagogy. A thorough understanding of the experience of performance should provide the basis to create a new framework for understanding the ways that ensembles interact and, ultimately, make music together.

Chapter 4
The Process of Performance

Reflecting upon the ways in which ensemble interaction has been examined thus far, it may be proposed that musicians can somehow articulate qualitative musical information regarding variables such as tempo, dynamics, intonation, phrasing and interpretation to their fellow musicians without engaging in intentional communication. The next step in this investigation is to examine the phenomenon of musical performance itself in an effort to determine where the qualitative information articulated by musicians may originate. The effect of individual musicians' performances on their coperformers would not be so important but for the underlying fact that both musicians and their performances are idiosyncratic. In recent years, the impact of musicians' individuality on the resulting performances has been increasingly emphasized. In his book *Authenticities* (1995), Peter Kivy proposes that performance should be considered a different species of artwork from the 'performanceless work' (1995: 279), a form of art that utilizes the performer more as an arranger than as a messenger (Ibid.: 283). The recognition of performance as a unique art form has prompted recent research on the methods by which musicians construct personal interpretations (Hellaby, 2009) and the extent that audiences may identify differences between interpretations (Gingras et al., 2008). Whilst there remain specific aspects of the construction and expression of individual interpretation in performance that require further exploration, it is accepted that musicians' decisions within performance directly impact the resulting musical work.

From this standpoint, we may consider the third research question: To what extent does the musical content being performed affect the ways it has to be physically created by musicians? Given that the performer affects the music being played, in what ways may the inverse apply? This chapter explores these questions by first delving into the psychology of intention and examining the process by which musical intention is aurally realized. To understand this process, it is necessary to consider psychological research on goal representation in simple and complex actions. This subsequently includes a discussion on the role that internal mental representations play throughout learning processes and in expert performance. Learning processes found in musical pedagogy include not only the cultivation of this form of mental representation, but also the training of musicians' bodies to carry out complex motions precisely and effectively. This discussion recalls the distinction made between Mode 1 and Mode 2 knowledge in the previous chapters of this book, examining how practical knowledge is both assimilated into and embodied within the performer. It is from this perspective that it becomes possible to examine the effect musical intentions have upon the resulting physical motions necessary in performance. A thorough understanding of the phenomenon of musical performance in this manner will provide the basis for a more holistic view of the ways performers' actions may be interpreted by other musicians.

Intention and Action in Musical Performance

In order to analyse the constituent aspects of musical performance, it is necessary to establish the underlying processes by which performers' musical intentions are physically manifested as sound. As this chapter is concerned with the processes by which individual musicians interact with their instruments, the ensuing discussions will accordingly focus on personal intention – that which pertains to individuals' mental objectives when performing actions. However, musicians' personal intentions are only one aspect of the phenomenology of performance. Chamber ensembles incorporate the actions and intentions of multiple musicians simultaneously, raising further questions of how intentions may be attributed to or shared amongst more than one person. This distinction between personal and attributed intention is particularly important in light of questions of unintentionality. Whilst there is an inherent disparity between what others may perceive to be intended and what actually is intended, lack of intention does not negate the fact that an action occurred. Hence, even when the process from intention to resulting action is not fully complete, the action itself will inevitably remain. That being said, the attribution and sharing of intention may only be fully addressed through an understanding of personal intention and therefore must be relegated to Chapter 5.

From Intention to Action

Michael Tomasello et al. define personal intention as 'a plan of action [an] organism chooses and commits itself to in pursuit of a goal, [including] both a means (action plan) as well as a goal' (2005: 2). These means and goals are hierarchical in that subsidiary intentions may be nested within overarching intentions (Powers, 1974). This structure is almost recursive in nature in that the means to achieve a certain goal is, on a lower level, a goal itself. Tomasello et al., commenting upon the embedded nature of multiple intentions, remark that:

> in general, what is a goal when viewed from beneath is a means when viewed from above. Starting at any given level, moving up to more general goals explains *why* a person has a particular goal … Moving down the hierarchy to more specific action plans specifies *how* a goal is achieved in terms of intentional actions. (2005: 3)

For the purposes of this book, personal intention may be considered to take one of three forms: intention for the future, intention of action and intentional action. The last two have particular relevance to musical performance. Recalling how musical information draws upon experience hearing and performing music, I propose that the basis of musical intention within performance is the decision to aurally create specific musical elements. Note that this form of musical intention is bound to the context of performance itself. Although it is certainly conceivable for other personal intentions to exist, such as the desire to win an audition or to provide a teaching example (as has been discussed in previous chapters), these personal intentions may be better classified as developmental or pedagogical rather than strictly musical. Therefore, for the present purposes, a performer's musical intention is the collection of qualities or characteristics they intend to embody within their musical output. As will be discussed further within this chapter, this intention may include both conscious and unconscious components residing within an overarching recursive hierarchy.

The first of these two forms of intention, the intention with which a musician acts, may itself be understood on various levels of detail. The most general form of this intention, presumably, would be simply to perform on an instrument. However, merely creating a performance is not usually sufficient for trained musicians; it is not enough for the performance to merely exist, but it needs to exhibit certain qualities or characteristics.[1] Therefore, the intention with which a musician acts may be understood as the desire to perform in a certain manner. Considering performance as the creation of aural output (at its very least), intention of action pertains to the musical parameters that make that aural output aesthetically desirable. These may include the intention to perform in a certain historical style, the intention to imitate a certain musician (coperformer or otherwise), the intention to be utterly unique, the intention to precisely execute the notated score, and so on.[2] These intentions of action are not mutually exclusive as they may describe different aspects of a performance: expressing one intention may not necessarily negate another. For example, the desire to imitate another performer does not mean that a musician has to forsake the qualities that make their performance individual and unique. Within a musical context, intention of action is comparable to performative interpretation and develops in a similar manner. Individual performative interpretation has been described by Julian Hellaby as emerging from nine 'informants': era (style), authorship (score), genre, topic, topical mode, characterizer, tempo, duration manipulator and sonic moderator (2009: 30). To varying degrees, these factors may influence the parameters that musicians decide to express or adhere to in their performances. Whilst this chapter will not dwell on the creation of interpretation at this point, it is important to recognize interpretation as a form of intention, as it serves as the set of characteristics that a musician desires a performance to embody.

---

[1] Recall the prioritization of the artistic object within presentational performance as described by Turino (2008).

[2] On the most fundamental level, this form of intention may be considered the intention to play certain pitches and rhythms. However, this is rudimentary when discussing musicians who are beyond the formative stages of learning to play their instrument.

Given the relationship between intention of action and musical interpretation, how may a specific interpretation be executed? It is one thing to intend to play a piece with a certain set of characteristics, yet quite a different one to actually do so. From this distinction rises the difference between intention of action and intentional action. Whereas intention of action pertains to the end product of an action, intentional action encompasses the range of subsidiary actions called for when executing the larger action: ancillary actions performed consciously or unconsciously. Considering the difference between these two concepts, the following discussion will focus on the relationship between mind and body, drawing upon the branch of cognitive research specifically pertaining to how humans execute intended actions.

The processes involved in intentional action are generalizable across a range of human activities, extending from button pressing to more complex actions such as sports (Kunde et al., 2004). However, it is not the actions themselves that are important but their subsequent results, referred to within psychological literature as action effects.[3] Birgit Elsner and Bernhard Hommel propose that action effects are the motivating factors behind actions themselves, writing that 'intentional action requires, and is actually controlled by, some anticipatory [mental] representation of the intended and expected action effects' (2001: 229). The cognitive presence of these action effects is vital to voluntary action (Ibid.: 230); thus, one can only truly intend to execute an action if they know what that action may result in. Although the parameters may be flexible, a mental correlate to both the intended action and its outcome is required. Individual musical practice provides a context to examine intention and action effects. In this case, intention is related more to the process than the product. Hence, a musician may intentionally experiment with their instrument's methods of sound production yet not intend to create the resulting sound. Once they attempt to replicate that sound, the actions required to do so will then become intentional. Given this, it is important to remember that the progression from action to outcome is never completely guaranteed. Whilst there is a direct (albeit not necessarily one-to-one) relationship between intention of action and subsidiary actions, intentional actions may result in multiple outcomes. Musical performance provides a context within which intentional actions could be considered to be entirely subservient to the intention of action (the goal, to use Tomasello's terminology). However, although the actions necessary in instrumental performance are undertaken primarily for the sake of the resulting sounds, these actions may indirectly achieve other outcomes. Recalling the conclusions Davidson and others have arrived at regarding the importance of visual elements of performance to audience perception, performers' actions may serve multiple purposes. Although musicians' actions may occur with the intention of creating sound, they may also indirectly fulfil other subsidiary objectives such as dramatic expression or explicit communication between coperformers.

---

[3]   See Elsner and Hommell, 2001; Kunde et al., 2004; and Schack and Tenenbaum, 2004 for discussion of action effects within the field of psychology.

Extending their research on action effects, Elsner and Hommel propose that the causal relationship between intentional actions and the effects of those actions is distinct from that assumed in most associative learning theories. Rather than creating mental associations between cause and effect in the direction it was acquired (cause before effect, when considered chronologically), they claim that 'whenever a stimulus follows a movement in time, the representations of the two events will be associated such that reperceiving the stimulus will tend to activate the movement. Hence, we assume [and have demonstrated] backward conditioning' (Elsner and Hommel, 2001: 239). This concept of 'backward conditioning', confirmed in subsequent literature, is now known as the ideomotor principle. Joachim Hoffmann et al. write that the ideomotor principle assumes that 'the anticipation, the mere idea of the desired effects, calls forth those motor activations that have previously been experienced as producing the desired effects' (2004: 347). Originally developed in the nineteenth century, this approach to understanding intentional action was discarded by the behavioural researchers of the early twentieth century only to gain a resurgence of interest in the past few decades (Ibid.: 347). Within the field of cognitive psychology, the ideomotor principle contributes to the theory that internal representation is a necessary part of the human perceptual-cognitive control system (Schack and Tenenbaum, 2004: 343). The following discussion will explore how the ideomotor principle may provide an explanation for intentional actions, both in musical and nonmusical contexts.

The Ideomotor Principle in Action

As examples of the ideomotor principle, consider the following two scenarios. Within this discussion, the specific actions undertaken are minor compared to the relationship of those actions to their intentions:

- A child throws a ball to her brother, who is standing 10 feet away from her. After catching it, he throws the ball back to her.
- A trombonist is playing in an orchestra. After playing his first note at a *forte* dynamic, the conductor asks him to play softer. The trombonist subsequently plays the same note at a *piano* dynamic.

Whilst different in a variety of ways, both circumstances provide examples of actions that, when manipulated, produce markedly different outcomes. Application of the ideomotor principle to these scenarios illuminates some of the physical and cognitive processes taking place. In the first scenario, it may be assumed that the children's goal in throwing the ball is not to articulate their anatomy in a particular way, but to allow their sibling to catch the ball. The ideomotor principle allows us to assume that the children implicitly understand that in order to achieve a given effect, they need to execute an appropriate action. Through experience moving objects through space, with gravity, and with the physical qualities of the ball being thrown, this reverse causal relationship can become increasingly nuanced.

Altering the events of this scenario, the girl will have to use markedly different physical actions to throw the ball should she move further away from her brother. Whilst throwing a ball maintains some similarities regardless of the distance covered, physical changes are necessary to compensate for different action effects. Therefore, specific characteristics of intention modify the actions needed to achieve the intended result.

Now consider the scenario involving the orchestral trombonist. Playing the instrument at *forte* and *piano* both require common elements: moving air through the instrument, maintaining a certain embouchure, keeping the slide at a precise length and so on. However, as volume is directly related to the amount of vibration through the instrument, differing dynamics require the trombonist to interact with his instrument in very specific ways. Although the physical differences when playing across dynamic ranges are nuanced, they are by no means negligible. All it takes is a small change in air speed for a *piano* to erupt into a *forte*, as any wind player stifling a laugh will know. All acoustic instrumental families depend upon subtle physical interactions in order to produce the wealth of musical sounds common in Western art music (Dahl, 2006: 129 and Windsor, 2011: 46). The relationship between movement and sound is ingrained in the act of playing an acoustic instrument, for, as Thomas Jerde et al. write, 'it is hardly surprising that one can predict a horn player is going to play something louder because she takes a large breath' (2006: 82). However, I propose that this ostensibly obvious relationship plays a significant role in the phenomenology of performance. A reverse causal relationship similar to the one seen with the children throwing the ball exists when musicians play their instruments; implicit understanding of this relationship allows intention to determine action.

The ecological understanding that moderates the relationship between action and effect falls firmly within the realm of Mode 2 knowledge. The children do not need to propositionally understand or communicate how they know how to throw a ball different distances, yet they do so innately. Consider if one attempted to teach this skill to a robot or some other entity reliant entirely upon Mode 1 knowledge. Although it may execute the action correctly, the robot would need to base its motions on accurate measurements of distance, weight, wind speed, and so on. Calculating the forces required to move the ball through space is simply a mathematical task should these variables be measured. However, the robot could not convert the experience of throwing the ball into the Mode 2 knowledge the children utilize. Likewise, it would be irrelevant to the children what the exact distance between them would be – they would simply throw the ball. Should it miss, they could adjust their actions with each subsequent repetition. Moreover, the children's minds may be optimized to function in this manner. Sverker Runeson and Gunilla Frykholm propose that 'evolutionary pressure has been on achievement, not on the kinematic detail of how we achieve. Therefore our motor system need not deal in movements as such – only in actions' (1983: 593). That being the case, even once the children have achieved the exact combination of movements necessary to throw the ball precisely, it is unnecessary for them to be aware of those individual movements. Instead, they are concerned that the ball goes where they want it to and that doing so feels a certain way.[4] This does not mean that the children are always unaware of their muscle movements, only that these individual movements do not have to be concentrated upon to occur.

The same principles are demonstrated in the case of the trombonist. In musical performance, action effects primarily take the form of sonic output. Whilst this may appear trivial, it highlights an important point that may be lost when applying cognitive psychology to performance studies. Sofia Dahl et al. comment that the effectiveness of musicians' actions when operating their instruments is continuously gauged in terms of the sounds the instrument produces, rather than the movements themselves (2010: 37). Similarly, Marc Leman notes that skilled performance involves treating an instrument like 'an extended body part', allowing musicians to focus on the aural output of their actions rather than the actions themselves (2010: 130). Thus, performers' action effects may be considered not only what I have previously called musical intention, but as the musical result itself. In this way, the intention to produce music that embodies certain characteristics will directly influence the manner in which a performer physically operates their instrument. This is possible through musicians' understanding of the mechanics by which individual performance functions, derived from extensive experience performing on and listening to their instrument.

I propose that engagement with this form of understanding within performance qualifies as a form of thinking. Some performers may not agree with the proposition that they 'think' while they play. However, I would argue that this objection is more semantic than anything else. In this case, 'thinking' is not necessarily the same conscious thought associated with Mode 1 knowledge; likewise, it is not characterized by linguistic expression, nor should it have to be. Rather, my use of the term 'thinking' is merely one of the ways to describe active engagement with knowledge, conscious or otherwise.[5] As Gilbert Ryle writes, overtly intelligent actions 'are not clues to the workings of minds; they are those workings' (1949: 57).

Although this analysis may appear to oversimplify the complexities of playing an acoustic instrument, I propose that this dynamic physical relationship between performer and instrument holds true for more subtle circumstances. Production of unique timbres, articulations and other expressive features relies on an intuitive understanding of the way in which the performer's body and instrument interact. The rationale behind this model is rooted in the processes inherent in individual practice and the development of instrumental technique. The following video

---

[4]   Runeson and Frykholm go on to propose that it may be impossible for the brain to operate in such a compartmentalized, controlling manner, saying that 'there cannot be … a motor program or a central controller instructing the myriad muscles in detail as to what they should do at each movement, simply because the magnitude of such a task would exhaust the capacity of any conceivable controlling device, brain or computer' (1983: 593).

[5]   I would like to express thanks to Christopher Redgate for insightful discussion on this topic.

examples, taken from performance and rehearsal settings, highlight the ways musical intentions may affect the relationship between performer and instrument. These examples progress from basic causal relationships between action and sound to increasingly complex correlations.

The first video example is taken from an improvised performance by The Supergroup.[6] Throughout Video Example 4.1, the bassist, Sebastiano Dessanay, interacts with his instrument in three distinct manners; he draws the bow across the strings in a traditional manner of performance, he plucks the strings and he strikes the back of the instrument's body with his hand. The fact that each of these techniques produces different sounds is hardly surprising; as many a contemporary performer knows, the search for 'non-traditional' techniques of instrumental sound production is ever ongoing. On a basic level, however, they illustrate that performers' sound-producing gestures directly correlate with the resulting musical output, recalling the four categories of physical gestures made during performance presented by Jensenius et al. (2010). Sofia Dahl et al. similarly describe how 'distinct sound properties' are directly related to specific movements used in the playing of instruments (2010: 46). Therefore, this video demonstrates how the type of sound-producing gestures executed may directly create a specific type of sonic output.

Given this relationship, what may be extrapolated about qualitative aspects of gestures and their resulting sounds? If a specific characteristic of a sound-producing gesture is changed, yet the overall structure remains the same, how will the music be affected? Video Example 4.2 explores this through an increase of dynamics across several instruments. This video, taken from a rehearsal of the second movement of Samuel Barber's *String Quartet No. 1*, was analysed in Chapter 2 with regard to communication. The present analysis is concerned instead with the performers' interactions with their instruments instead of with their fellow musicians (see Example 4.1 for the corresponding excerpt from the score).[7]

Performing the *crescendo* in this excerpt results in increased movement by the cellist and violinists, particularly on their ascending two-note motif. Although the *crescendo* is indicated in their parts, the performers' physical movement (intentional or unintentional) exists whether or not the players are true to the score. A dynamic relationship between musician and instrument provides one explanation for the violinists' and cellist's increased motions at the end of this video. Execution of louder volume requires performers' bows to move faster across the strings of their instruments, necessitating faster bodily movement. Having developed extensive experience playing stringed instruments, the performers of the Boult Quartet understand the relationship between action and sonic output and can consequently adjust their actions to play at a certain dynamic. Whilst this brief analysis only considers the effect of physical motion on volume, the possibility exists that more

---

[6]   *Improv.*, Birmingham Conservatoire, 19 January 2011: *Waltz of the Tearing Tears*.

[7]   Material from this discussion developed from a presentation I gave at the Performa'11 Conference on Performance Studies at the University of Aveiro, Portugal (May 2011).

Example 4.1 Samuel Barber, *String Quartet No. 1, Op. 11*. Movement II, bars 35–40

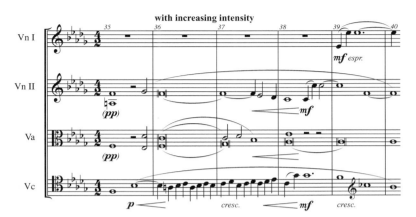

qualitative aspects of performance, such as articulation or expressive modification of timing, are similarly related to physical action.[8]

The next video example allows for investigation of whether even more nuanced musical elements than a change of dynamics or pitch may motivate changes in performers' sound-producing gestures. Consider the excerpt found in Video Example 4.3 (see Example 4.2).[9] Specifically under scrutiny is the way that the violist interacts with her instrument changes when playing contrasting musical content. In this play-through, the violist's movements at the beginning of the excerpt are slow and measured. However, on the third beat of bar 16, her physical motions noticeably change. At the beginning of her moving crotchet line, she applies more bow pressure in a faster motion. This results in diagonal bodily movement from the lower right to the upper left side of the performer. The stillness of the musical line around it causes this motion to appear distinct and even slightly out of place.

Analysis of the score may highlight factors that may motivate the violist's change in motion. As opposed to the previous example, however, the change in musical output does not appear to be overtly tied to a change of musical instruction. In fact, cursory examination of the viola part shows that there is a written *decrescendo* before the moving crotchet line. Strict application of previous

---

[8]   Additional support for this conclusion is found in pedagogical literature. For example, Edward Kleinhammer's *The Art of Trombone Playing* (1963) and Scott Whitener's *A Complete Guide to Brass* (1997) describe in detail the physical elements necessary to produce certain articulations and tone qualities on brass instruments.

[9]   Material from this discussion has developed from presentations I gave at the Royal Musical Association Postgraduate Students' Conference at the University of Manchester (January 2011) and the Performa'11 Conference on Performance Studies at the University of Aveiro, Portugal (May 2011).

Example 4.2   Samuel Barber, *String Quartet No. 1, Op. 11*. Movement II, bars 15–18

conclusions may prompt the assumption that as the viola line gets softer, the necessary motions should diminish accordingly. However, the opposite occurs. Why does the violist change musical intentions so dramatically from what is indicated within the score? Within this musical context, the crotchet line serves as a countermelody, pulling the viola away from its previous accompanimental role. By performing the countermelody with such sensitivity and awareness, the violist illustrates her recognition of the musical roles found within this movement. Whether this shift in prominence derives from analysis of the score, prior discussion or a spur-of-the-moment decision, the violist is likely engaging in *knowing-in-action*. Donald Schön describes this form of knowledge as appearing 'in much of the spontaneous behavior of skillful practice' in a manner that 'does not stem from a prior intellectual operation' (1983: 51). The past experiences of the violist, both as a listener and as a performer, allow her to make informed decisions regarding her musical intentions. Considering performance as a form of skilful practice, complete with its own form of knowing-in-action, suggests that musicians' decisions are informed not only by 'intellectual' (that is to say, propositional) influences such as score-based analysis, but also experience in performance itself: the application of Mode 2 knowledge. This experience includes highly individual aspects of performance, such as knowledge of how a certain instrument responds in a specific register, or broader elements, including conventions of orchestration such as melody, countermelody and accompaniment.

Within all of the examples discussed thus far, the physical changes made by the performers to reflect differing musical intentions are all observable. The differences in action that take place may differ radically in terms of proportion and extent; Sebastiano turning his bass around is certainly more noticeable than the Boult Quartet violist's slight adjustment of torso movement. Even so, the musicians' physical changes and their aural effects can be perceived by observers. Naturally, changes made within a musician cannot be directly observed. I would be hard pressed to tell from visual inspection whether a fellow trombonist was placing their tongue at the back of their teeth or at the roof of their mouth. However, as they performed using that specific articulation, the effect of their physical actions would be evident aurally.

The observable changes of musicians' actions while performing may provide insight into how their musical intentions have changed as well. Interpretation of these changes, however, requires experiential knowledge on the part of the observer, a topic that will be examined in the next chapter. For the current discussion, however, it is useful to consider a circumstance where the causal relationship may be most evident to an observer: the beginning of a musical phrase. At this point in a performance, musicians are in the preparatory stages of action, priming themselves to operate their instruments. This involves not only anticipatory mental representation of specific action effects, but also the physical positioning of their bodies so they can execute subsequent actions. For example, in order to produce sound on a wind instrument, performers need to blow air through their instrument, and consequently need to inhale before playing. This preparatory breath is influenced by a combination of the performer's action-effect representation and procedural knowledge of how to operate their instrument; that is to say, in order to execute X action effect, Y and Z physical actions need to occur. The physiological adjustments required before physical action occurs have been referenced in the literature on kinematics as preadjustments. Runeson and Frykholm, when describing a person carrying a heavy box, remark that 'to be efficient, postural adjustments must often be undertaken before a new activity is begun. Hence, postural preadjustments, tuned to the intended action, are characteristic constituents of animal activity' (1983: 590). Therefore, considered purely from an individual performer's perspective, preparatory actions allow the musician to be in the best possible position to execute their musical intentions. The effect that preparatory actions (beats, breaths, up-bows or otherwise) have on the resulting sonic output has been expounded in both pedagogical and anecdotal literature. Michael Tree, violist with the Guarneri Quartet, comments that preparatory gestures 'should always be at one with the spirit of the music, whatever it may be ... When a movement starts lyrically, the preparatory beat should often seem more a continuation than a beginning' (Blum, 1987: 13). Similarly, Mine Dogantan-Dack argues that 'it is not the exquisite phrasing that follows the [singer's] breath, but the breath that follows the singer's (embodied) mental conception of the musical phrase' (2006: 461). Pedagogic accounts from my own education stress the importance of breathing in the spirit with which I intend to play. Whilst preparatory actions have the potential to affect coperformers, the present discussion will be limited to the effect that preparatory actions have on the individual performers themselves. Their capacity to effect ensemble interaction may circumvent the traditional avenues of communication discussed in Chapter 2, and will be examined further in this book.

It is worth noting that as the relationship between musician and instrument becomes more complex, it increasingly resists expression within the discourse of Mode 1 knowledge. A basic causal association between action and effect in music, such as observed when Sebastiano played his bass in three different manners, may be easily indicated linguistically. Written scores are often littered with performance directions to interact with an instrument in a certain manner, a trend that has increased throughout the twentieth century.[10] However, linguistic indication of more complex associations between the performer and their instrument – which may subsequently result in timbral or interpretative changes in the resulting music – fails for two reasons.[11] First, whilst there are undoubtedly common techniques used when playing instruments, details of these techniques quickly become idiosyncratic. Although all trombonists play using common motions, differences in our physiology necessitate that we interact with the instrument in slightly different manners. This is the case even with performers who were taught by the same instructor or in the same pedagogical ideology. Dahl et al. write that 'since the combination [of movement] possibilities [in performance] are so numerous, it is likely that many different movement strategies can result in the same sound event' (2010: 37). Therefore, a notated instruction directing a musician to operate their instrument in a highly specific, subtle manner may have inconsistent musical results across a variety of performers. Second, whilst musical elements such as tempo, form, articulation and volume may be easily represented graphically, elements such as timbre, character and expression resist representation in a non-aural format. Consider score indications such as *maestoso*, *affettuoso* and *con fuoco* – descriptors that, although common, are not quantifiable elements of a performance to the same degree that tempo, form, articulation and volume may be identified. As was discussed previously, the terminology used to describe these musical elements is forced to rely upon metaphor to convey the desired effect instead of the action. Thus, performance indications that allude to the relationship between performer and instrument in order to create a specific musical element may be forced to rely on metaphoric language.

The presence of descriptive text within scores implicitly attests to the boundary between Mode 1 and Mode 2 knowledge. Instead of describing how the performer should interact with their instrument, such as an indication to turn a bass around and strike its back with a hand, it is more effective to describe what the resulting music should sound like. From there, the performer may determine (consciously

---

[10]   For example, string players are familiar with techniques such as *pizzicato* and *sul ponticello*, brass players with *con sordino* and so on. Extended techniques have become increasingly common and varied throughout the twentieth century, ranging from Mahler's indications to raise the bell of a brass or woodwind instrument above a performer's music stand (*mit aufgehobenem Schalltrichter*) to Crespo's indication that a trombonist rapidly move their slide in and out its entire length (*Schnelle Zugbewegung von der 1. zur 7. Position unabhängig der Tonhöhe*).

[11]   This critique does not extend to situations where musical performance is conceived as a matter of theatre. In such circumstances, linguistic description of performers' actions may arguably be the best way for the score or instructions to be notated short of providing a video demonstration of those actions.

or unconsciously) the best method by which that sound may be achieved. The distinction between propositional and procedural knowledge here is not abstract. It would be overwhelming to perform from a score filled with technical descriptions of how to physically play a piece of music. Current notation depends on the use of verbal and graphic metaphors and symbols whose effective interpretation is bound to performers' experiential knowledge. In this way, the boundary between Mode 1 and Mode 2 knowledge is reified through the profound effects it has upon the ways musical notation and practice evolve.

The examples discussed throughout the first half of this chapter demonstrate the inherent causality not only between action and effect in instrumental performance, but more importantly the intimate relationship between intention, action and effect. The intention to create a certain musical effect – be it a specific timbre, volume, expressive interpretation, and so on – alters the actions required to physically produce that effect. That being said, the relationship between musician and instrument proposed in this chapter may not be explicitly understood by performers. More importantly, given its reliance upon Mode 2 knowledge, this relationship may not have to be understood in a propositional manner at all. In the next section of this chapter, I will investigate how comprehension of the dynamic relationship between musician and instrument may become a form of embodied knowledge, retained in such a manner that it does not have to be consciously recognized to be effectively used. This requires reflection on individual practice and instrumental pedagogy. From there, I will be able to identify the constituent aspects of embodied knowledge in solo performance.

Developing Embodied Knowledge

Skilled solo performance necessitates the tacit understanding of the relationship between musical intention, action and resulting sonic effect.[12] Most commonly, development of this understanding is not through trial and error (as if someone were creating or discovering an instrument in a social vacuum), but through instruction and individual practice. These processes augment and structure the experience of learning to play an instrument so as to encourage the acquisition of procedural knowledge. Musical intentions are embodied in the sense that they are 'actually part of, or [make] use of, the sensorimotor system of our brains' (Lakoff and Johnson, 1999: 20, emphasis removed). Lakoff and Johnson's definition of embodiment reifies what may be considered abstract internal representations of musical elements. However, as will become more apparent, musical performance is inherently physical, experiential and ultimately embodied. This section

---

[12]   This section focuses on the establishment of instrumental technique rather than the acquisition of fundamental musical skills such as aural acuity and temporal awareness. For further information on these subjects in relation to child development, see Shuter-Dyson and Gabriel, 1981.

investigates how instrumental pedagogy and individual practice develop Mode 2 knowledge in performers.

Blending Modes Of Knowledge: Instrumental Pedagogy

The utilization and development of action-effect representations have been implicitly stressed in pedagogic approaches to instrumental performance. These mental correlates of sonic events include fundamental relationships between pitches and rhythms: the structural elements that underlie Western art music. Whilst these structural elements also provide the basis for a host of methods by which music may be propositionally analysed (c.f. Lerdahl and Jackendoff, 1983), the importance of mentally 'hearing' what one intends to play is affirmed by examination of undergraduate programmes of study, which often include at least two years of aural skills training. Through exercises in recognizing increasingly complex pitch relationships and rhythms, aural skills classes are designed to cultivate finely tuned mental imagery – imagery that plays a large role in conceiving nuanced musical intentions.

Across the spectrum of pedagogical approaches, it is worth noting that instrumental instruction requires a blend of Mode 1 and Mode 2 knowledge. Recalling Schön's proposal that skilled practice cannot be conveyed to a novice 'merely by describing [the art's] procedures, rules and theories', nor can the novice 'think like a seasoned practitioner merely [through descriptions or demonstrations of expert] ways of thinking', lack of experience within the 'media and language of their practices' creates a barrier to understanding (1983: 271). Within instrumental instruction, aspects of the experience of performance need to be described through the use of Mode 1 knowledge. At early stages of instruction, it is necessary for students to explicitly know *how* to operate their instrument. The instructor may then critique students' playing and correct any discrepancies. As students accumulate experience, they will accordingly acquire Mode 2 knowledge. Beyond the increasingly intimate understanding of the relationship between action and effect in instrumental operation, this form of knowledge includes most importantly the ability for self-critique – not only skill in recognizing what is aesthetically desirable, but also reconciling disparities between musical intention and resulting sonic output. Through supporting each other in this manner, Mode 1 and Mode 2 knowledge are not mutually exclusive: which is the cart and which the horse depends entirely on circumstance.

Even while an instructor conveys propositional knowledge to their student, they also actively engage the student in the practice of talking about music. As mentioned in the previous chapter, rehearsal language develops from experience playing and listening to music. Similarly, the teacher – enculturated into the 'media and language of [musical] practice' – not only represents musical elements through metaphor, but by doing so actively cultivates the student's musical imagination. Through the development of new, idiosyncratic metaphors for musical elements, the teacher trains the student not only in the ability to play an instrument, but to create suitable metaphoric correlates to musical intentions. Therefore, musical instruction includes both the propositional knowledge necessary to the physical production of sound on an instrument (knowing *how* to use the instrument) and the ability to engage in multimodal musical discourse. Whilst the scope of this book must be limited to this brief discussion on the relationship between Mode 1 and Mode 2 knowledge within instrumental pedagogy, I hope that the ensuing conclusions may inspire a further critique of how modes of knowledge are handled within musical teaching techniques.

Ever-increasing Intimacy: Individual Practice

Individual practice is the means by which fluency on an instrument is achieved, an essential element of the acquisition of musical skill (Barry and Hallam, 2002: 152).[13] Resources such as technical exercises (scales, arpeggios, articulation and phrasing studies, and so on), études (including lyrical or character studies) and specific musical excerpts from solo, ensemble or orchestral literature, are used to refine nuances of instrumental performance. The impetus for this incessant struggle for perfection can be found in the underlying motive for presentational performance in general – not only to produce sound, but to manifest a performer's musical intentions. Therefore, practising increases one's ability to fluently and accurately articulate the qualities that characterize a specific musical intention. Nancy Barry and Susan Hallam describe practice as enabling 'complex physical, cognitive, and musical skills to be performed fluently with relatively little conscious control, freeing cognitive processing capacity for higher order processing' (2002: 155). Deficiencies in, or inordinate concentration on, playing technique may hinder the effectiveness of what a musician is trying to aurally present.[14] This process of sensory response and behaviour modification has been described by Tor Halmrast et al. as both an auditory-motor feedback loop and a motor-haptic feedback loop (2010: 207; cf. Cadoz and Wanderley, 2000, Palmer, 2006 and Zatorre et al., 2007). These feedback loops are vital to the learning process as they establish the relationship between physical action and sonic effect.

---

[13]   For the purposes of this book, I include the voice as an instrument. Whilst acknowledging the differences between instrumental and vocal performance in terms of process, the similarities shared in overall methods of pedagogical development and the acquisition of skill are enough to treat them as the same for the current discussion.

[14]   A phrase anonymously passed around through one music department I attended was 'Analysis causes paralysis', alluding to both the crippling effects of not being 'in the moment' while performing and the mysticism that often surrounds the acquisition of an expert skill. Of course, analysis (be it theoretical, performative, historical, and so on) may be useful in preparation for performance. This phrase was more likely referring to the kind of propositional analysis that may also remove a musician 'from the moment', disrupting a flow state.

From a technical standpoint, practice allows for increased familiarity in the causal effect between the way an instrument is operated and the resulting aural output. Peter Keller and Iring Koch demonstrate that increased experience playing an instrument 'may promote proficiency at action-effect anticipation by improving one's ability to engage in auditory imagery' (2008: 282). Likewise, further research has shown that 'auditory imagery ability improves with increasing musical experience' (Pecenka and Keller, 2009: 285). The feedback from the instrument to the performer allows the performer to produce more accurate auditory imagery, which in turn allows for more specific goals to be set during performance. After learning the difference between what it felt to play *fortissimo* and *piano* in my own musical development, I could apply that causal relationship in more nuanced ways. This eventually allowed for a wide spectrum of dynamics to be at my disposal in performance. Likewise, I could only gain proficiency over articulation, expression, intonation, and so on through prolonged experience with my bass trombone in a variety of performance situations. Thus, as experience with an instrument grows, the relationship the performer has with it and with the music being played becomes increasingly intimate.

Similarly, individual practice allows performers to become familiar with the idiosyncrasies of their particular instrument. Within each instrument, variations in construction and sound production create opportunities for performers to draw out a myriad of timbres, tones and volumes. It is not uncommon for musicians to comment on the playing characteristics of an instrument using metaphoric terminology not dissimilar to that used in rehearsal (for example, 'this trombone has a very bright sound', 'I love how cleanly this mouthpiece lets me articulate', or 'the heaviness of that horn creates a rather velvety sound'). Likewise, musicians may refer to differences between makes and models of instruments in terms of how they 'feel' to play as much as how they sound. In this circumstance, when a musician plays an instrument that 'feels' different to them, their learned understanding of the physical causation between action (instrument operation) and effect (sound produced) does not sufficiently transfer to a new instrument. Although general trends will be the same – they should be able to create some sounds on the instrument – the nuanced relationship between the performer and the instrument will have to be re-established in order for them to be fully comfortable. Looking beyond the qualitative differences between makes of instruments, each specific instrument itself contains unique, individual subtleties in tone production. Tor Halmrast et al. describe this phenomenon in the following manner:

> Some points [on a percussion instrument] have a high impedance for higher frequencies and react very strongly to lower ones, some points are driven easily for higher frequencies and not so good for lower ones. In terms of gestures, this entails a different reaction of the body of the percussion instrument to the striking mallet or stick. (2010: 205)

Whilst the generalized use of the term 'gesture' understates the relationship between physical motion and sound produced, this statement corroborates with the proposed model of performer–instrument interaction detailed thus far in the chapter.

In addition to increasing fluency in performance, individual practice encourages musicians to develop flexibility in mental focus. When beginning to learn how to play an instrument, basic skills of tone production are necessary before more advanced musical techniques are addressed. As these basic skills are acquired and refined, less attention needs to be paid to them, allowing attention to be focused elsewhere. The process of assimilating smaller actions and skills into larger mental units allows Keller and Koch to describe performance as involving the execution of 'prelearnt sequences of movements on an instrument to produce auditory effects' (2008: 275). Through the acquisition of a skill, the subsidiary actions required for that skill become subsumed into the skill itself. Davidson describes the ability for a performer to shift their focus through 'large amounts of practice and experience' as the ability to 'play without conscious attention to the thoughts and actions used in the production of the performance' (2002: 144). Marc Leman examines this process further, considering the instrument as 'an extended body part' that allows the performer to 'focus on the goals of the sound-performing gestures rather than having to focus on the execution of the sound-performing gestures on the mediator' (2010: 130). The assessment of sound-producing gestures is therefore conducted in reference to resulting sounds rather than specific 'characteristics of movement' (Dahl et al., 2010: 37). The children playing catch, discussed earlier, judge the merits of each throw by the results of that throw, rather than analysis of the specific motions used while throwing. One might argue, on the other hand, that professional baseball players would pay close attention to the details of their actions when throwing. However, as in music, athletes are presumably more focused on successfully completing a certain play rather than analysing what their musculature is doing. This is not to say that such scrutiny does not take place in the practice of skilled musicians or athletes, but that it is more appropriately relegated to individual practice and rehearsal instead of performance. In performance, this reflection may only effectively occur *post hoc*. Recalling Csikszentmihalyi's concept of flow (1990), skilled practice requires a directness and immediacy between intention and effective action – qualities that are achieved through individual practice. Conscious reflection within a performance may provide cognitive interventions that remove one from a flow state. The balance of challenge and skill achieved in flow may be disrupted when a musician cognitively removes themselves from their performance situation in order to critique specific elements of that performance. Whilst this disruption may not necessarily cause any issues within the practice room, it may incur negative effects during performance.

As performers develop proficiency on their instruments, they fine tune the associated physical actions required (Nirkko and Kristeva, 2006: 189). Effective operation of an instrument is the means by which performers can express specific musical intentions. However, the relationship between musical intentions and consequent physical motions may not simply be dependent upon the feedback loops developed through practice. As seen in the previous example of the Boult Quartet's violist, aspects of performance such as familiarity with orchestration, ensemble balance and characteristics of repertoire can not only affect the sounds produced by a musician, but also the physical motions needed to create them. All of these factors play a role in developing a form of musical knowledge based firmly within Mode 2. Through the clarification of factors that contribute to the accumulation of embodied knowledge, we can approach the question of ensemble interaction from a perspective built upon the performance phenomenology of individual musicians.

Conclusion

Thus far in this book, I have developed the proposal that musical performance requires and engenders a unique form of understanding. Emerging from the experience of performance itself, such understanding may be 'separate from prior intellectual operation' (Schön, 1983: 51). Consequently, it does not have to be consciously recognized to be effectively used. I propose that the knowledge utilized in musical performance is inherently embodied. Strictly speaking, embodied knowledge is that which develops out of bodily experience (Godøy, 2010: 105). Ikujiro Nonaka and Georg von Krogh (expanding upon the work of sociologists such as Maturana and Varela) describe this knowledge as 'intuitive, tied to the senses, and escaping any formal analysis through self-introspection' (2009: 642). As seen through investigation of the development of knowledge through individual practice and teaching, it appears appropriate to classify the understanding a musician has regarding the relationship between them and their instrument as emergent from bodily experience.

Given the importance of physical experience in embodied knowledge, what role may 'non-physical' experience play? Is it possible for other elements of experience to inform embodied knowledge? Recall again the third example of the ideomotor principle in action, involving the violist in the Boult Quartet. Through experience practising and performing, she has accumulated extensive knowledge of how she interacts with her instrument – knowledge that may be incontrovertibly described as embodied. However, this development has not existed in a vacuum. She is not only a performer, but also a listener; as remarked earlier, her performance is influenced by a variety of sources, not the least of which is her relationship with her instrument. It is only through understanding musical elements and conventions such as melody, harmony, orchestration, ensemble balance, characteristics of repertoire, expressive phrasing, and so on that her tacit understanding of how her instrument works may be appropriately contextualized. Whilst these musical elements may need be propositionally taught to nascent performers, a nuanced understanding of them can only be developed through their experience with musical works. Therefore, embodied musical knowledge is not only rooted in the experience of performance and listening, but also the comprehension of the relationship between the two. Musicians exercising knowledge during a performance may not consciously think about the process of playing, but think in such a way that engages with their musical intentions, the musical elements in the piece (past, present and future) and the feeling of creating specific musical elements with their instruments. Just as Kivy argues that listening to a performance and recognizing musical characteristics such as phrasing, inversion and stretto illustrates how listening is a 'conscious cognitive activity' (2007: 228), I propose that musical performance requires engagement with a form of knowledge emergent from experience as a listener and performer.

In this chapter, I have attempted to identify the most generalizable elements that constitute the phenomenology of solo performance, regardless of the instrument being played. The resulting model integrates the performer's intention to aurally create specific musical elements with their embodied understanding of their instrument's operation. Recalling that the intention to create a certain musical effect alters the actions needed to physically produce that effect, musicians implicitly understand the dynamic relationship between their musical intentions (action-effect representations) and the processes needed to aurally reproduce the associated musical elements with their instruments. This understanding evolves through experience with the instrument itself and the social contexts of individual practice, instrumental pedagogy, rehearsal and performance. The embodied musical knowledge promoted by this model falls firmly within the realm of Mode 2 knowledge.

From this revised perspective of the phenomenology of performance, we may examine the influence of embodied knowledge within ensemble performance. The complexities inherent in aurally manifesting musical intentions are compounded when considered within the context of musical ensembles, where intentions may be attributed and shared amongst multiple people. Likewise, the simultaneous unfolding of numerous diverse performances may provide a catalyst to the development of interpretation. The final research question of this book escalates our present understanding of the phenomenology of performance to a higher degree of intricacy, interrogating how the physical relationship between a performer and their instrument may relate to the communicative and interactive processes of ensemble performance. Through this examination, we bring together the final pieces through which a new paradigm of musical interaction may be proposed.

Chapter 5
Reaction and Inter-reaction

The discussions that have taken place throughout the previous chapters have established three vital points in relation to ensemble interaction within Western art music. First, the application of a communicative paradigm does not sufficiently describe the complex processes by which performers can share musical intentions with each other. It is therefore necessary to rethink the underlying framework upon which ensemble interaction is based, with the intention of creating a new framework that does not rely solely on the process of intentionally encoding information. This is not to say that explicit communication does not occur within ensemble interaction, but that it does not fully account for the richness of interaction present. Second, musical performance requires the implementation of a specific kind of Mode 2 knowledge. This knowledge is based upon extensive experience creating and listening to music. Out of this knowledge emerges a wide range of flexible metaphors to describe musical elements in terms of other realms of experience. However, there still remain questions as to how this knowledge may be exercised within ensemble performance. Third, performers' musical intentions influence, to varying degrees, the way they have to operate their instruments. In performance, there is a correlation between intention (interpretation) and action (the process of instrumental performance).[1] The intimate relationship between performers and their instruments demonstrated in the previous chapter has thus far only been considered in terms of individual performance. Out of these conclusions, this chapter will consequently focus on the fourth and final research question: How does the physical relationship between the performer and their instrument relate to communicative and interactive processes of ensemble performance? The application of conclusions found within this book will provide the context within which a new paradigm of ensemble interaction may be developed.

This chapter will begin by reframing our present understanding of embodied musical knowledge within a larger social system: an unconducted musical ensemble. Discussion thus far has considered embodied knowledge in relationship to individual musicians' experiences as a performer and listener. Ensemble performance, on the other hand, engages musicians within a larger sphere of contextual elements with which to interact. The question of how embodied

---

[1] A correlation between intention and action does not mean that musicians are free from making mistakes. Whilst increased fluency on a musical instrument (the ability to consistently execute a musical intention) decreases the likelihood that a performer will make a mistake, humans are not infallible. However, it is beyond the scope of the present discussion to investigate why and how mistakes occur in musical performance.

knowledge may be exercised within an ensemble setting prompts a continuation of the previous chapter's discussion on intention. This discussion expands beyond personal intention to encompass intention as perceived by observers and shared by collaborators. It is therefore necessary to explore the attribution of intention through inference, a topic that may have multiple implications within this book. In combination with current musicological theories regarding the interplay between improvising musicians, it will then be possible to construct a new framework for ensemble interaction. I will critique this new paradigm in the following chapter, exploring some of the possible ramifications it may have from the perspectives of both musical researchers and practitioners.

Contextualizing Embodied Knowledge

Reflecting upon discussions found in the previous chapter, embodied knowledge has three primary characteristics. First, embodied knowledge develops out of bodily experience. This form of knowledge, 'constantly shaped by our experiences', forms the basis of humans' 'instinct, urges, and unconscious reactions' (Jones et al., 2009: 167). Second, and more specifically, embodied knowledge is intrinsically 'tied to the senses' (Nonaka and von Krogh, 2009: 642). Mental activity alone is not enough to embody a certain element of knowledge; such mental activity accompanies and may be instigated by physical action. Third, embodied knowledge is intuitive, 'escaping any formal analysis through self-introspection' (Ibid.: 642). Its acquisition and retention is not confined to propositional reflection or expression, placing it firmly under the auspices of Mode 2 knowledge. Considering myself as a bass trombonist, it is possible to create a generalized understanding of what embodied musical knowledge may encompass in relation to instrumental performance.[2] In light of the three characteristics summarized above, my bodily experience includes a wide variety of musical situations, each of which may impact on my musical intentions in different ways. Experiences as a professional musician and casual listener contribute to my understanding of the mechanics and internal logic by which music operates, at least within Western art music. It is important to note that these mechanics are not necessarily analytical in nature. Whilst propositional analysis of music certainly contributes to my overall knowledge, it is only through experience seeing, hearing and feeling that propositional knowledge in practice truly becomes embodied – the second characteristic of embodied knowledge described above. In this manner, propositional knowledge is folded into experiential knowledge.

---

[2]   I do not intend to limit the scope of embodied musical knowledge simply to instrumental performance. It is conceivable that such Mode 2 knowledge may be manifested in different manners, through listening, composing or dancing. As this book focuses on ensemble interaction, I leave open the possibility of other aspects of embodied musical knowledge to be explored in further research.

Godøy's proposition that 'music perception is multimodal in the sense that we perceive music with the help of both visual/kinematic images and effort/dynamics sensations, in addition to the "pure" sound' (2010: 106) may be too simplistic; is musical perception truly additive in this manner? Rather, a musician's experience while performing may be considered multimodal in that it engages multiple senses at once. Physical resonance from the instrument and the sounds occurring from other sources in the performance, visual elements and, naturally, the sound itself contribute to haptic, visual and aural feedback to the performer (Michailidis and Bullock, 2011: 227). The understanding I have of the performance experience is such that it is unable to be directly translated into a linguistic, spatial or graphical format. Whilst I may (and commonly do) create metaphors with which to articulate specific elements of performance, the experience of performance itself may not be fully described propositionally. This becomes most apparent when I teach trombone, combining Mode 1 descriptions of physical details (such as how the tongue operates during articulation or how hand positions affect operation of the instrument) with metaphors of Mode 2 concepts (such as how I approach shaping different musical phrases or create my own interpretation).

To what extent may these characteristics of embodied knowledge remain similar when considering ensemble musicians? The implementation of an individual's embodied knowledge of instrumental performance may encourage the development of procedural knowledge necessary for effective ensemble interaction.[3] Godøy suggests that an understanding of the processes underlying instrumental operation, when applied to listening, encourages 'ecological' knowledge. This form of knowledge is acquired 'through massive experience of sound-sources in general and musical performances in particular' (2010: 106). However, he describes ecological knowledge not from the perspective of a performer but from the point of view of listeners in general:

> in listening, we see a whole range of relationships between sound and assumed sound-producing gestures, ranging from the immediate and synchronous (and probably hard-wired) coupling of sound-event to action-event, to the more interpretative and holistic coupling of sound-event to action-event, and even to the projection of non-existent action-events into sound-events. (Ibid.:107)

Therefore, when an individual sees and hears a musician performing, they can correlate between the perceived sound-event and action-event. For example, a fundamental association may be made between a trombonist putting the instrument to their lips and the ensuing sound. As an observer gains more experience with this specific musical sound and the action-events necessary to create it, they can then further distinguish more nuanced relationships between sound and action.

---

[3]   Material from this discussion developed from a presentation I gave at the Centre for Musical Performance as Creative Practice Performance Studies Network International Conference at the University of Cambridge (July 2011).

Beyond simply identifying an instrument as the sound's source, a more complex relationship would be to differentiate between instruments, identifying that it is more likely that the sound of a trombone will be created by a trombonist than by a violinist. Conversely, further experience would allow the observer to identify the instrument that creates a sound purely from an aural recording, without drawing upon any visual information. Knowledge of the correlation between action-event and sound-event is brought into stark relief through parody and comedy in music. Jokes, as noted by Kivy, 'rely on a stock of knowledge or belief, and feeling common to the teller and hearer' (2003: 6). Musical humour subverts listeners' expectations because those expectations (what Godøy (2010) refers to as ecological knowledge) commonly exist. Musicians such as Victor Borge and Anna Russell can therefore draw upon and manipulate audiences' expectations of how instruments work and the conventions found within classical music. Likewise, comedic elements of Luciano Berio's trombone solo *Sequenza V* (1966) would not be considered funny should the audience not have sufficient ecological knowledge. Thus, humour in music demonstrates the existence of some form of musical knowledge.

Godøy's concept of ecological knowledge appears to serve as an extension of the understanding of embodied knowledge explored thus far in this book. However, the term 'ecological' may not be the most accurate description of this form of knowledge. The term 'ecological' implies that such background is innate in the human condition and recalls the similarly labelled approach to perception developed by cognitive psychologist J.J. Gibson.[4] This ecological approach to perception is considered 'direct in the sense of not entailing inference or similar constructive operations on insufficient input data' (Runeson and Frykholm, 1983: 586). However, it is the lack of 'inference or similar constructive operations' that suggests that the 'ecological' may not be the most suitable descriptor of the form of embodied knowledge that emerges from the 'massive experiences' Godøy describes, as it appears that the knowledge he proposes precedes inference. Likewise, whilst the ability to correlate a sound to its source may be a hard wired cognitive function,[5] to what extent can advanced stages of this ability be considered fundamental? Individual experience must play a role in the degree to which this ability is developed. John Dewey proposes that experience is:

> a matter of the interaction of organism with its environment, an environment that is human as well as physical, that includes the materials of tradition and institutions as well as its local surroundings. The organism brings with it through its own structure, native and acquired, forces that play a part in the interaction. (1934: 256)

---

[4]   Runeson and Frykholm (1983) provide an overview of this literature, which specifically references Gibson's publications of 1950, 1966 and 1979.

[5]   For an overview of this subject, see Blauert, 1983.

Instead of considering such knowledge to be instinctive, therefore, it may be more appropriate to consider the innate *potential* of every living organism to 'read' information in its environment and adjust behaviour accordingly. Lakoff and Johnson argue that all neural beings have evolved an ability to categorize as a matter of survival (1999: 17). However, whilst the kind of knowledge that Godøy proposes is an advanced form of categorization, its complexity and richness arise from an individual's experiences. Instead of referring to this developed mode of categorization as ecological, I propose that Dewey's term 'environmental' may be more appropriate. Rather than existing in humans from birth, environmental musical knowledge develops out of one's experience within contextual conditions. Therefore, it may emerge from the specific circumstances and events experienced by an individual, prompting them to engage with some form of conscious or subconscious inference.

The model of environmental knowledge proposed by Godøy does not address the extent to which the ability to correlate sound-event to action-event may be refined. It is one thing to simply correlate a sound to its origin and another thing to infer qualitative information about that sound source from its sensory output. Given that expert instrumentalists accumulate a large amount of embodied musical knowledge, how much information could be inferred about the relationship between sound-events and action-events? Likewise, what kind of information may actually be inferred? Marcelo Wanderley and Bradley Vines write that 'clarinettists' movements, including their facial expressions, postures, breathing and effective gestures, augmented audiences' experience in three ways: (1) by reinforcing the information available in sound; (2) by contributing unique information to the overall experience; and (3) by conveying the performer's musical interpretation of the score' (2006: 180). However, this research does not reveal what 'unique information' may be expressed by gestures, nor the relationship between gestures used and the musical interpretation produced in the performance. In order to address the application of embodied musical knowledge within the ensemble contexts, it is necessary to examine the topic of inference in musical performance. This will extend the previous chapter's discussion of personal intention to the realm of attributed intention, exploring the elements that contribute to one's ability to assume intention on behalf of another's actions. Consequently, this discussion will examine how humans may infer information from observed physical motion. From this standpoint, it will be possible to address how a combination of embodied musical knowledge and inference may contribute to ensemble interaction in a way distinct from existing communicative processes.

Inference

The questions posed in the previous section pertain to the overarching issue of inference. Within this book, inference may most appropriately be identified as the assumption of the mental or physical state of another person. Specifically, inference of mental states involves deducing qualities of an other's personal intentions through observation of their actions when executing those intentions. In relation to ensemble performance, this is comparable to the assumption of a someone's musical interpretation while they are performing. However, these musical intentions (which, as forms of Mode 2 knowledge, resist linguistic articulation) may only be accessible through the sensory traces that accompany their performance. Therefore, in order to address how personal intentions may be attributed or shared, it is necessary to understand how interior mental states can be observed. This section of the chapter will consequently focus on three areas. The first explores how humans can infer information about the mental and physical states of another through visual and aural observation of that individual in action. An understanding of how humans receive information through multi-sensory channels will then allow for a discussion of how intentions may be perceived, attributed and shared. The third area of this section contains the application of these cognitive theories to the inference of performers' musical intentions. From this perspective I will establish how musicians can infer information from their fellow performers and the content of that information itself.

The Kinematic Specification of Dynamics

Before addressing the complexities that arise when considering the processes of attributing or sharing intentions, it is important to remember that playing an instrument is not purely a mental activity such as making abstract decisions. The inherent physicality of performance suggests that it may be subject to some of the same underlying processes that govern other bodily actions. Research on kinematics has shown that humans can infer a large amount of haptic information purely from visual input.[6] Runeson and Frykholm demonstrate that observers can accurately gauge the weight of a box by watching someone pick it up and carry it (1981: 733). Those watching the individual holding the box could identify how heavy or light the box was simply through the way that the person had to interact with it. Therefore, the authors write that:

> if information [about relevant dynamic properties] is available in the kinematic pattern, it is also available as higher order properties of the optic array, thus making direct visual perception of dynamic properties possible ... When objects get involved in events some of their hidden properties are disclosed. Vision is therefore likely to have a role in what is usually taken to be the privileged domain of the haptic sense. (Ibid.: 733)[7]

---

[6]   I would like to express my thanks to Elaine King for bringing research on kinematics to my attention.

[7]   In this area of motion research, kinematics focuses on 'displacement, velocity, and acceleration' whilst dynamics pertains to motion from a causal perspective (Runeson and Frykholm, 1981: 733).

Within this experiment, the 'hidden properties' of the box primarily had to do with its weight – something that cannot be gauged purely through visual observation of the box. Thus, the importance of visual observation in the determination of objects' physical properties becomes evident when actions occur involving those objects.[8]

Further research by Runeson and Frykholm identifies the principle that 'movements specify the causal factors of events' as the kinematic specification of dynamics (1983: 585). They explain that this principle's importance within human perception in that we do not perceive movements as abstract manifestations of physical forces, but rather 'we perceive causal aspects of events' (Ibid.: 588). Whereas a computer may interpret a person carrying a box in terms of the physical qualities of the system, humans focus instead on determining the physical elements that explain the causality of the system (such as deducing that the box had to be held in a certain manner *because* it was heavy). This leads the authors to argue that 'the kinematic pattern of a person in action by mechanical, biological and motor-control-related necessity is rich in information about both permanent and transient properties of the person and what he or she is in fact doing' (Ibid.: 598). Therefore, Runeson and Frykholm identify 'what a person is actually doing' as one of the primary qualities which may be expressed through kinematic display (Ibid.: 609).

Application of the kinematic specification of dynamics to musical performance presents an intriguing approach to answering one of the questions posed in Chapter 2: how do musicians share information while performing? As discussed in the previous chapter, there is a direct relationship between the way musicians interact with their instruments and the resultant sounds. The variety of physical approaches used when operating musical instruments will often lead to kinematic changes – differences in motions that may be observable to viewers. This does not necessarily entail that these kinematic changes will be significant to an arbitrary observer. However, it does mean that performers' interactions with their instruments may potentially serve as a source of information to onlookers.

To explore this proposal, recall the examples of the children playing catch and the orchestral trombonist provided in the previous chapter. This time, however, we will consider these examples as if someone was observing each situation. In the first scenario, what information may an observer infer from the way that the girl throws the ball? This question closely mirrors research by Runeson and Frykholm in which participants are asked to deduce how far an actor threw a small sandbag upon observation of just the major joints on the actor's body (1983: 598). The authors conclude that the onlookers can effectively determine the trajectory and resultant distance of the sandbag without having seen the sandbag itself. Returning to the children playing catch, it is therefore possible to determine how far away

---

[8]   The importance of visual observation is not limited to interactions between humans and inanimate objects. In earlier research, Runeson describes how the kinematics of a linear collision between two objects may provide insight about those objects' physical properties to observers (1977).

from each other they are standing based upon the way that each child throws the ball. Likewise, this information may be available to observers before the ball is actually thrown. As noted in the previous chapter, postural preadjustments play an important role in the preparation for physical activity (Ibid.: 590).

Now consider the overly enthusiastic trombonist. Due to the relationship between performer and instrument, the trombonist needs to play his instrument in a certain manner in order to produce a *forte* dynamic. This physical approach differs from that which is required to execute softer dynamics particularly in regard to the embouchure, air speed and quantity of air necessary. Extension of Runeson and Frykholm's conclusions regarding postural preadjustments illustrates that differences in kinematic approach are not only observable during performance of a note itself, but before that note is actually played. Therefore, the way in which the trombonist prepares to play provides visual evidence for the resulting sonic output. Inference of distinct musical effects from physical causes in this way will be explored in depth later in this chapter.

Whilst at first glance it may appear straightforward to infer basic qualities of sound through observations of musicians, questions remain as to how nuanced this ability may be. It is one thing to infer that a trombonist is going to play because they put their instrument to their lips and quite another to deduce that the resulting musical sound will display certain characteristics. Although the kinematic specification of dynamics provides an understanding of the method by which musicians may perceive musical intentions, the implications of attributing or sharing intentions among individuals requires further exploration. The next section will examine how cognitive research on the perception of intention may apply to ensemble research. From this perspective, it is possible to propose how inference within performance may operate – a concept that provides the basis for a new paradigm for ensemble interaction.

Shared and Attributed Intentions

In the previous chapter, discussion of intention focused upon the relationship between an individual's goals and their requisite actions. Within a social group, however, focus shifts away from whether or not personal intention and ensuing actions correspond correctly with each other. Instead, two other themes emerge: the effect of aligning intentions between group members and the process by which observers may infer intentionality to the individual's actions. These themes address not only how intentions may be interpreted by observers, but also the impact that the personal intentions may have on those around the individual. After briefly reviewing each of these avenues of inquiry, this section of the chapter will examine how these topics may be applied to musicological research on ensemble performance.

Personal intention, as discussed in the previous chapter, primarily consists of 'a plan of action' carried out 'in pursuit of a goal' (Tomasello et al., 2005: 2). In musical performance, this goal could range from simply producing sound on an instrument to playing in a very specific manner, corresponding to the performer's higher-level musical intentions. Within an ensemble, however, new goals are incorporated. Herter Norton writes that 'chamber music is a social enterprise, the nucleus of sympathetic gatherings wherein the players are depending upon each other for the achievement of their common interest' (1925: 5). This 'common interest' includes cohesiveness and coordination between the performers, particularly in terms of such variables as timing, intonation and interpretation – important attributes that contribute to what may be contextually appraised as a successful ensemble performance in Western art music. Out of these individual actions and goals emerges a phenomenon known as shared intentionality. Tomasello et al. describe this state as the 'collaborative interactions in which participants have a shared goal (shared commitment) and coordinated action roles for pursuing that shared goal' (2005: 6; citing Gilbert, 1989, Searle, 1995 and Tuomela, 1995). Emphasizing both a 'shared goal' and 'coordinated action roles', this form of intentionality resonates with the view of ensemble interaction proposed within this book. Beyond simply recognizing this form of intention, Tomasello et al. examine how shared intentionality may affect how individuals work together. Reminiscent of the discussion in Chapter 2 about alternating leadership, they propose that:

> the cognitive representation of the intention also contains both self and other …
> This is necessary because both collaborators must choose their own action
> plan in the activity in light of (and coordinated with) the other's action plan …
> [requiring] that each participant cognitively represent both roles of the
> collaboration in a single representational format – holistically, from a 'bird's-
> eye view,' as it were – then enabling role reversal and mutual helping. (2005: 7)

Therefore, recognition of shared intentions between collaborators shapes the roles they bear. Through a constant give and take, ensemble members can assume varying amounts of leadership in light of the group's overarching goals. Arnold Steinhardt, first violinist with the Guarneri Quartet, refers to this process when he comments that 'most of us would like to have chances to lead in some respects while being content to follow in others. There's a harmonious balance in life when you can slip in and out of roles. Quartet playing provides that kind of variety' (Blum, 1987: 154). Shared intentionality may thus answer a question posed in Chapter 2: how do ensemble performers achieve fluidity of ensemble roles without verbal interaction? Through the recognition of shared musical intentions, musicians can conceive an ensemble's goals in a 'single representational format'. The consolidation of goals and required actions into a cohesive cognitive unit allows ensemble members to gauge the extent to which their individual actions impact on the end result of the group's performance and modify their role accordingly. Reflecting upon my experience within chamber ensembles, this proposal appears accurate. The more I know of what is happening beyond my part within an ensemble, the more effectively I can assess and fulfil my role within the group. The ability to shift roles is based not only on my understanding of musical conventions such as melody, harmony and orchestration, but also my evaluation of the present group context: neither of which require verbal interaction with my coperformers. This recalls an example from the previous chapter, in which the violist of the Boult Quartet emphasizes a moving line although there is no explicit instruction in the score to do so (see Video Example 4.3 for the rehearsal footage and Example 4.2 for the corresponding excerpt from the score). Her change in musical role may be rationalized through her and her fellow musicians' understanding of the importance her line plays within the overall performance. Whilst the concept of shared intentionality may provide an answer to the question of how musicians may assume *ad hoc* leadership positions while performing, one primary question needs to be attended to. Without explicit notification of a performer's musical intentions, how may their fellow musicians determine what those intentions are? Therefore, it is necessary to overview the process by which intention may be perceived by and attributed to individuals.

Recent research on the philosophy of intention extends investigation of attributed intention into the realm of ethics, questioning the moral implications of placing blame on perceived intentional action.[9] However, the positive or negative interpretation of another person's actions may not be directly applicable to ensemble performance, although particularly dysfunctional chamber groups may succumb to the deteriorating effects of their members' paranoia and suspicion of each other. On a fundamental level, however, the attribution of intention is necessary when attempting to infer meaning or significance from others' actions. Stanley Fish argues that 'it is impossible *not* to construe [intention] and therefore impossible to oppose it either to the production or the determination of meaning' (1989: 100). He continues this thought in one of his later essays, where he comments that people 'cannot help positing an intention for an utterance if they are in the act of regarding it as meaningful' (Ibid.: 116). Therefore, inference of meaning within one's actions requires the assumption that the person observed is acting intentionally.

Within ensemble performance, attributing intention is most connected to gauging the successfulness of an individual's performance – successfulness in the sense of whether or not that performer accurately and effectively manifests their musical intentions. Consider the scenario below.

The flautist and clarinetist in a traditional Western classical wind quintet are rehearsing a passage in which they are scored in unison octaves. The first time they play through the passage, the two musicians play almost all of the same notes with the exception of the final pitch; instead of a note one octave lower than the flute's, the clarinetist plays a seventh lower. The second time they play the passage, the same thing happens, resulting in a seventh rather than an octave.

Given that the quintet members have noticed this discrepancy, they may interpret the event in a variety of ways. If they were to interpret the event as meaningful, various levels of intention may be attributed to the clarinetist. Negatively, the

---

[9]   For an overview and examples of this literature, see Hindriks, 2008 and Knobe, 2004, 2006.

quintet members may assume that the clarinetist is unaware of the mistake, as it was repeated without correction – the clarinetist may be intentionally playing that note, but unintentionally playing incorrectly. In order to rectify the situation, the incorrect note would have to be brought to the attention of the clarinetist. In a positive manner, the quintet members may assume that the clarinetist was intentionally playing the note that was written in the part. The incorrect note may be purely the result of an ill-copied part instead of a playing error. If the quintet members did not assign meaning to the event, however, the issue of intention may not arise at all. Had the note been fixed the second time the passage was played, the other musicians may have passed the mistake off as accidental, assuming that the clarinetist was aware that the note was incorrect. The error would consequently be understood to be unintentional. Similar situations have developed traditional practice for English cathedral choirs. Should a chorister sing incorrectly and they raise their hand, the director is aware that the singer knows they made a mistake. However, should they sing incorrectly and not raise their hand, the director knows that they were unaware of the mistake and may need additional rehearsal. Widespread use of this practice suggests how useful the distinction between conscious and unconscious mistakes are for musical directors.

These scenarios, whilst useful in giving examples of how musicians may interpret their coperformers' actions, only deal with the repercussions of a missed note. What about situations where there is no explicitly 'correct' or 'incorrect' manner of playing? If a musician phrases a melody in a certain manner, adds a different inflection, plays slightly louder or softer, or modifies any other qualitative variables of a performance, their coperformers have to decide whether or not those modifications are intentional and, accordingly, meaningful. The attribution of intention (therefore meaning) may correlate to the amount and quality of information that musicians can conclude from their coperformers' actions.

Inferring Musical Intentions

As the preceding discussions have shown, humans infer information about others' intentions and goals based on the actions used in accomplishing those goals. Within performance, those intentions may be highly complex combinations of musical attributes that, when combined, constitute what is commonly referred to as a performer's interpretation. As musicians become more skilled (both in terms of instrumental technique and aural acuity), the individual intentions that compromise their interpretations may become increasingly detailed. To what extent may such intricate interpretations be inferred by observers? As explored in the work of Runeson and Frykholm, varying amounts of information may be inferred based not only upon the actual events being perceived, but also the background of the observers:

> perception requires not only potential information but also corresponding attunements of the perceptual system. Informational specificity is not to be

equated with perceptual saliency ... Depending on property concerned and activity observed, person-and-action perception may range from the simple noting of the obvious to requiring the utmost of educated attention. (Runeson and Frykholm, 1983: 598)

Therefore, the amount of experience an observer has with the elements being perceived directly impacts on the amount and kind of information they can infer through observation. More intricate than Runeson and Frykholm's examples of box-lifting and sandbag-throwing, musical performance is a complex action that requires 'the utmost of educated attention' to fully interpret. 'Educated', in these circumstances, does not refer to propositional Mode 1 knowledge. Instead, it is rooted in the experience 'of sound-sources in general and musical performances in particular', to borrow Godøy's (2010) terminology, directly correlating to the embodied musical knowledge described in previous chapters. Colwyn Trevarthen et al. write that 'our movements communicate what our brains anticipate our bodies will do and how this will feel because others are sensitive to the essential control processes of our movements, which match their own' (2011: 11). Thus, the greater familiarity a musician has with a certain context (be it a specific instrument, style of playing, ensemble composition, and so on), the more information they may infer through observation of a performance (Jäncke, 2006: 27).

This proposed correlation between environmental, embodied musical knowledge and the amount and kind of information inferred through observation is corroborated in my ensemble experience. As a bass trombonist, I can make nuanced inferences about other trombonists' performances based upon the musical knowledge I have developed through practice and performance. The conclusions I may arrive at when watching and playing with other trombonists encompass a variety of categories, from predicting the style, quality and volume of sound to be produced based upon a breath to determining how tired or nervous they may be. These conclusions, rooted in direct experience with my instrument, demonstrate my idiosyncratic understanding of how to play a trombone (as opposed to other musical instruments). The understanding I have of the way I need to operate my bass trombone in order to achieve certain sounds as well as what happens when things go wrong strongly influences the information I can infer from another trombonist's performance.

The extent to which my experience affects the amount of information I may deduce from coperformers becomes strikingly prominent when I am placed within various ensembles. Within a brass ensemble, I can extrapolate a large amount of information regarding musical variables due to my accumulated understanding of how brass instruments work. That said, I am not normally cognizant of the extent to which this background affects the way I function within an ensemble. However, the following example illustrates the potential effects of a lack of environmental knowledge. One of the requirements for my Masters of Music in chamber music at the University of Michigan was to organize and perform in a recital consisting of mixed chamber ensembles. Along with a sonata with piano, a low brass trio (described at the beginning of this book) and a brass quintet, I included the concert suite version of Igor Stravinsky's *Histoire du soldat* (1918). The work is scored for a septet of violin, bass, clarinet, bassoon, cornet, trombone and percussion. Although all of the musicians I asked to play in the septet were familiar with performing with mixed instrumentations (particularly with symphony orchestras and wind bands), the variety of instruments performing together provided unique challenges to ensemble interaction. Likewise, the orchestration of the piece often pairs together instruments that may not traditionally share melodic lines. Although each musician was accomplished in their own right (and recognizing the difficult nature of Stravinsky's writing), the piece was difficult to put together as an ensemble. Whilst we could often play the correct notes in time with each other, it was apparent that everyone was, to varying degrees, out of their performing 'comfort zone'. As our familiarity increased with both the mechanics of instruments different from our own and the individual performers within the group, the ensemble became accordingly more cohesive and integrated. Although extensive individual practice assuredly contributed to the development of our final performance, the effect of increased familiarity between the specific performers and the kinds of instruments being played cannot be ignored. It comes as no surprise that experience, be it playing a certain kind of instrument, within a certain type of ensemble and even with certain musicians themselves has a dramatic effect upon how much meaningful information may be inferred.

It is important to distinguish this form of information as meaningful in order to distinguish it from a propositional taxonomy or classification of observations. Within this context, 'meaningful' refers to the richness of musical content that may only be alluded to linguistically through metaphor. Inference within performance, informed through embodied environmental knowledge, allows musicians to access their coperformers' intentions. This knowledge develops out of musical experience, both as a performer and as a listener. The kinematic specification of dynamics proves vital in establishing how musicians share information with each other through performance. Upon reflection, however, whilst the metaphor of 'sharing' information is appropriate, the direction of the flow of information needs to be reversed. Rather than performers 'pushing' information to one another, it may be more appropriate to consider them 'pulling' it. Thus, through inference, they can deduce their coperformers' musical intentions from the mere act of performance itself, although the word 'mere' understates the importance of this conclusion. This model emphasizes the richness inherent in the phenomenon of performance: richness in terms of multimodal sensory experience as well as in forms of knowledge engaged ('pulled') by performer and audience. Graeme Wilson and Raymond MacDonald note that musical events within improvising jazz ensembles may emerge as signifiers with 'the potential for multiple divergent meanings to be read into … by coperformers' rather than 'a straightforward transfer of meaning in the manner of the transmission model of communication' (2012: 565). Thus, it falls to observers to attribute intention and meaning to musical events.

Runeson and Frykholm's original proposal of the kinematic specification of dynamics emphasizes the role vision plays in perception and observation (1981: 733). However, human perception is not limited to sight. In musical performance, aural faculties play a primary role in the contextualization of experience. Although this may seem obvious given that music is a form of sound, it is important not to discount the role of aural perception in performance. Whilst sight provides one avenue by which musicians may infer their coperformers' interpretations, visual input *augments* aural input, and does not displace or override it. Highly skilled ensemble musicians may choose not to look at each other while playing and still present compelling performances. Although such musicians actively disregard visual input, I would argue that they are still observing their surroundings. Within musical performance, aural input is elevated to equal or higher status than the other senses due in part to its role in the final work of art and the immediacy with which it engages the human sensory system.[10] The observation of sound involves not simply its perception, but its identification and consequent attribution of importance, meaning or classification. It is one thing to aurally perceive a musical performance and another to observe the qualities that characterize that performance. Experience allows for increased epistemological identification of these qualities – a process aided through visual observation. Perception and identification of the visual elements of instrumental performance provide clarification of what is happening or what will soon happen aurally. Observation is therefore an amalgamated sensory experience within ensembles. Performers may infer information from a variety of sources, shifting between visual and aural input as necessary.

As has been explored within the first two sections of this chapter, the environmental knowledge acquired by musicians develops through experience within ensembles themselves, allowing them to 'read' their contextual environment. To what extent does the ability to infer information from situational context allow performers to adjust their subsequent behaviour? The next section of this chapter will explore how theories originally developed to explain elements of improvisation within ensembles may be applied to more nuanced aspects of musical performance. From there, it will be possible to assemble and critique a new framework of ensemble interaction.

Continuous Adaptation

This chapter has thus far addressed how embodied environmental knowledge can contribute to the information ensemble members may infer from their fellow

---

[10]   In his philosophical writings, John Dewey details the interaction between sight and sound, commenting that each provides specific elements to understanding one's environment. According to him, the immediacy of sound arises from its ability to physically resonate with the human body, although its origin is external (1934: 245).

musicians' performances. Although this is a key step in understanding how ensembles operate, there remains a further question with regard to inference. Presuming that chamber musicians infer qualitative musical information from the performances occurring around them, how may this affect how their interpretation of their own part is created? With each action taken within an ensemble, the feel and atmosphere of the group slightly alters. This subtle shifting creates new circumstances within which performers make interpretative decisions. Michael Tree, violist with the Guarneri Quartet, describes this flexibility as 'an organic process' in which 'each [musician is] influenced by constantly fluctuating circumstances. Every movement of our playing is conditioned by what has just occurred or by what we think is about to occur. It remains creative because just about anything can happen' (Blum, 1987: 20). Uniqueness and creativity thus emerge from the transient context created through joint performance.

Continually shifting ensemble conditions become apparent when considering the effects of inference, particularly in creating the context within which an appropriate reaction may be determined. Considering a nonmusical example, if one person physically collides with another while walking, the attribution of intention may lead to wildly different reactions. Should the second person not attribute intention (and thereby, meaning) to the first, the incident would be interpreted as a mere accident. However, should the second person believe that the first intentionally ran into them, the action could be regarded as a malicious shove. Within ensemble performance, the attribution of intention and meaning to actions may have a similar effect. Changes in interpretational contexts would therefore encourage musicians to react in different ways. In this vein, Tomasello et al. remark that the attribution of intention is necessary to ensuing action, concluding that 'the cognitive representation of the intention also contains both self and other … This is necessary because both collaborators must choose their own action plan in the activity in light of (and coordinated with) the other's action plan' (2005: 7).

In comparison to the communicative paradigm detailed in Chapter 2, the ability to 'read' the environment does not entail any intention to communicate on the part of an external agent. However, whilst intention may affect attributed interpretation (the difference between an accidental push and an ill-intentioned shove), intention does not change an action's existence. Whether or not either person *meant* to run into the other does not mean that the event did not happen. Recall that chapter's example of the Boult Quartet's cellist misjudging a bow stroke, thereby performing softer than in a previous play-through. Regardless of his intentions (or lack thereof), the cellist's bowing created a situation to which his coperformers had to react. This section of the chapter will examine the role of reaction within ensembles, a process that will provide the final piece of a new framework of ensemble interaction.

Attunement

David Soyer, cellist with the Guarneri Quartet, remarks that the key to spontaneous string quartet performance can be found in the 'reactive' nature of the ensemble (Blum, 1987: 20). This sentiment is echoed throughout practitioner and musicological literature on chamber music. Identifying ensemble interaction as a 'highly complex communicative exchange', Tovstiga et al. write that 'all musicians respond and react continually to the audible and visual impulses they are registering around themselves' in performance (2004: 9). More specifically, Kokotsaki proposes that musicians engage 'in a kind of active listening', which allows them to be involved in 'a process of musical adaptation whereby alternatively musical possibilities [are] considered in an open and flexible manner' (2007: 657). Each new element presented through an individual performer's interpretation provides a possible impetus for subsequent interpretations. Along these lines, Paul Berliner notes that 'while attending to their own parts – assessing inventive material and selecting elements for development – performers must constantly exercise musical peripheral vision to make similar assessments about neighboring parts as they endeavor to predict their courses' (1994: 364; see also Goodman, 2002: 156). Given these descriptions, it appears appropriate to extend Soyer's phrasing to describe ensemble interaction as both a 'reactive' and 'active' process. However, none of these testaments to the reactive nature of ensemble performance go into further detail as to how this process functions.

Based upon the descriptions cited above, fluidity of ensemble interaction may be the result of several common elements. First, there is an emphasis on musical information (that is to say, 'musical possibilities' and interpretations) simultaneously flowing to and from performers. This information, whilst constantly being transmitted to the ensemble members, does not have to be consciously or semantically encoded, thereby circumventing explicit communication as described in Chapter 2. Every action and sound made by a musician can be 'read' into by their coperformers, regardless of their intentionality. Robert Hatten touches on this by specifying gesture as 'any energetic shaping through time *that may be interpreted as significant*' (2006: 1; my emphasis), allowing for the possibility that unintentional or seemingly inconsequential motions may be regarded as important. Second, the exchange of information between performers is a result of aural and visual observation on the part of each musician. This takes the form of what Kokotsaki refers to as 'active listening' and the process that Tovstiga notes as musicians registering 'audible and visual impulses … around themselves'. Third, the interpretative changes prompted by constantly evolving musical contexts happen directly within performance. Reflection and action occur simultaneously, a detail noted by Soyer when he writes that 'everyone feels [a lead] at the same time; everyone is thinking towards a central point … We don't follow each other; we play together. There's a difference in that' (Blum, 1987: 15).

These common elements may be encapsulated within a process called attunement. Developed out of research on improvisatory jazz groups, Keith Sawyer writes that:

> group musical performance can only work when the performers are closely attuned to each other. They have to monitor the other performer's actions at the same time that they continue their own performance, to be able to quickly hear or see what the other performers are doing, and to be able to respond by altering their own unfolding, ongoing activity. (2005: 51)

That being said, it is not enough to simply register what the other performers are doing within an ensemble. Effective attunement requires that ensemble musicians accurately infer meaningful information from their coperformers. Equally important is the ability to distinguish between accidental and intentional actions, as reactions to these actions may then be modified based upon such a differentiation. However, as will be illustrated later in this chapter, the fact that a performance includes accidental characteristics does not mean that it may not encourage interpretative modification by other performers. As discussed above, musicians' comprehension of information inferred from their fellow performers takes the form of applied environmental knowledge. Thus, the embodied knowledge musicians acquire through learning and practising their instrument, in addition to the knowledge assimilated as performers and listeners, impacts on ensembles they perform in. This experience provides the cognitive resources by which they can make inferences about forthcoming sound-events based upon the perceived sounds and sound-producing gestures of their coperformers. The assimilation and application of environmental knowledge is alluded to by John Dalley, first violin with the Guarneri Quartet, when he writes that there is 'a certain body language that each of [the quartet members] has when he plays. You get to know that about your colleagues and react accordingly. Over the years a great deal of it becomes intuitive' (Blum, 1987: 14). Recalling previous discussions throughout this book, Dalley's statement illustrates how musical knowledge acquired, embodied and applied through ensemble interaction may encompass even the most idiosyncratic elements of individuals' performance styles.

Attunement is the means by which musicians' environmental knowledge may be effectively applied to ensemble interaction. Elaine King touches upon this process when she writes that 'ensemble performers carry out complex predictions that are intimately bound to reactions gained through feedback' (Goodman, 2002: 154). I would argue that the 'complex predictions' she speaks of build upon the richness of musicians' experiences, allowing them to infer their coperformers' musical intentions in a way that does not necessitate (and often evades) verbal articulation. Musical performance itself thereby provides all the information one needs to effectively deduce a musician's intentions – provided that there is enough experience to ground that inference.

The Paradigm of Inter-reaction

From this perspective, I can propose a new framework for understanding the process by which ensemble performers interact and share information.[11] This understanding of ensemble interaction draws extensively upon the wealth of Mode 2 knowledge skilled musicians have acquired and, I argue, continually apply through performance. Developed out of the conclusions reached within this text, this framework is based not on a paradigm of communication, but a paradigm of reaction. This framework consists of three primary stages: transmitting, inferring and attuning.

- *Transmitting*: The way a performer operates their instrument is dynamically related to their musical intention. The variety of nuanced techniques required for instrumental operation demand physical changes that may be discernible to an observer. Therefore, the execution of different musical intentions results in changes to the aural and visual output of a performer, changes that may be noticeable and even meaningful depending upon the experience of those persons perceiving the performance. Whilst this stage has been described within the paradigm of communication presented in Chapter 2, here it encompasses all sensory output of the ensemble performers, not simply that which has been deliberately encoded.
- *Inferring*: Through the use of embodied musical knowledge (acquired through extensive experience playing instruments, participating within ensembles, observing other performances and with general musical conventions such as melody, harmony and orchestration), skilled chamber musicians may infer their coperformers' musical intentions based on the sensory output they perceive. Depending on the degree to which the musician is familiar with the surrounding instruments being played and the performers themselves, conclusions may range from determining basic sonic properties such as volume and tempo to more nuanced shadings of interpretation and phrasing.
- *Attuning*: Within an ensemble, musicians perceive individual contributions to the performance occurring alongside theirs and draw conclusions about the implications of those contributions. In conjunction with the musical characteristics of these individual performances, chamber musicians apply the inferred musical intentions of their fellow performers to their own unfolding performance. Thus, they constantly modify and adjust their interpretation to recognize the ensemble's overarching, shared intentions.

Due to the cyclical nature of this process, I propose that this paradigm is rooted not simply in reaction, but more accurately in inter-reaction. Every action in

---

[11]   Material from this discussion developed from a presentation I gave at the Centre for Musical Performance as Creative Practice Performance Studies Network International Conference at the University of Cambridge (July 2011).

performance begets another, creating a socio-musical context that constantly adapts to the constituent members' musical interpretations.[12] Thus, ensemble performance is shaped not only by the individual musicians' interpretations, but their own continuously unfolding performances as well. By extension, inter-reaction describes how an ensemble may gain its own collective interpretative momentum – a state that performers refer to as the music 'playing itself'. The illusion of the music taking over the group may arise when musicians are so attuned to one another and the emergent performance that interpretative intentions become cognitively distanced from individual musicians. Instead of single performers alternately leading the ensemble, the balance of creative input and adaptation found in this seemingly magical performative state encourages a sense of cognitive freedom and flexibility. The creation of the ensemble's interpretation is distributed to such an extent that it may feel like the musicians are tapping into something greater than their individual musical intentions and acting as a unified whole. Total involvement in performance in this way is reminiscent of Csikszentmihalyi's concept of flow (1990) and the social unity of participatory music described by Turino (2008). Thus, inter-reaction may encourage the development of an ensemble flow state as well as a social sameness between performers.

This framework does not negate the possibility of explicit communication within ensembles. Rather, it removes an element crucial to communication, encoding, from the equation. The three stages of inter-reaction do not have to be predicated by either the intention to communicate or explicit encoding of an idea. Therefore, the paradigm accounts for *all* events that may transpire during a performance, rather than simply those intended to happen. The ramifications of this aspect of inter-reaction will be explored further in this chapter, clarifying what actions may be considered to be intentional and unintentional within musical performance.

One could argue that the disregard of the original performer's intentions within inter-reaction is hypocritical, given that the framework so prominently presumes intentional reaction on the part of the other musicians within the ensemble. However, such an argument inordinately focuses on the question of identifying the evolution of intention (as a mental concept) between ensemble members rather than the observable effects of those intentions. As stated before, the presence or lack of an intention for an action does not negate the existence of that action. The underlying premise of this framework is that observable reactions to events within performance may provide insight into musicians' intentions, rather than the other way around. The concept of musical inference, emergent from skilled musicians' embodied knowledge, provides the rationale by which attunement works so effectively and immediately.

---

[12]   The framework of inter-reaction appears ostensibly similar to the flow of perception and action proposed by Luke Windsor (2011: 60). However, Windsor's framework is only concerned with an individual performer or listener and does not go into the detail of how it may be applied within an ensemble.

Whilst inter-reaction appears to be a theoretically appropriate means of describing ensemble interaction, it is necessary to apply it to specific performance situations in order to confirm its validity. The next section of the chapter provides an analysis of three video examples of the Boult Quartet in rehearsal, including the excerpt that served as a foil to the paradigm of communication in Chapter 2. After examination of these examples, Chapter 6 will explore the implications of this framework on further research on ensembles, the semantics of performance vocabulary and the nature of musical knowledge itself.

Revisiting the Boult Quartet in Rehearsal

The first example to be analysed in terms of inter-reaction is Video Example 5.1. In this rehearsal, the Boult Quartet plays through an excerpt from the second movement of Samuel Barber's *String Quartet No. 1, Op. 11* (see Example 5.1 for the corresponding excerpt from the score).

Example 5.1   Samuel Barber, *String Quartet No. 1, Op. 11.* Movement II, bars 35–40

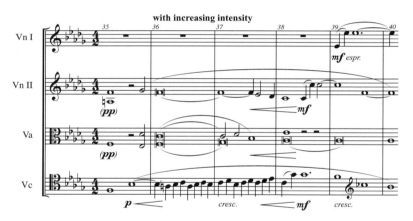

As remarked in the analysis found in Chapter 2, in this play-through the cellist uses a markedly smaller amount of bow at the end of his melodic line (bar 38) than he has previously. The second violinist reacts to this change of musical circumstance and accordingly plays his rising octave line softer than he has previously. Analysis of this event via the paradigm of communication does not sufficiently explain this occurrence, in that the vital process of encoding either does not happen or generates incorrect data. Similar analysis of this situation via inter-reaction does not require the cellist's intentions to be considered; whether or not the cellist intended to underestimate the amount of bow available to him does not matter. However, his doing so created a discrete situation (and accordingly, aural and visual output) to which the second violinist must react. The violinist, upon reception of this multimodal information, infers the resulting musical output of the cellist – a softer, less dramatic phrasing. Note that the focus here is neither on what the cellist intends to do, nor on whether the violinist can deduce the cellist's original underlying intentions. Instead, the violinist, applying the sensory information he perceived of the cellist's performance, reacts to the actions and resulting sounds he concludes are actually going to happen. Through attunement, he adapts his own musical plan to incorporate the qualities inferred from the cellist's performance, subsequently adjusting his own playing approach. This video therefore provides an example of how ensemble interaction may be considered to be continuous empathetic adjustment to simultaneous performances.

Although this video was taken from rehearsal, such accidents may also happen in live performance, regardless of how prepared or skilled the ensemble members may be. Musicians need to respond and react to their own 'errors' as well as those of their colleagues in the ensemble. This may not necessarily be unfavourable, as adept reactions to unexpected events are a highly valued aspect of live performance. The temporal essence of music as an art form encourages the idiosyncratic unfolding and evolution of each performance. In David Dubal's interviews with professional concert pianists, several musicians comment on how performing itself sparks interpretative development. Jorge Bolet remarks that 'freedom and spontaneity are what make music-making really interesting' (Dubal, 1985: 79). That spontaneity often occurs in seemingly unconscious situations such as those described by Tamás Vásáry:

> I love the improvisatory element of performance which interacts with my conception of the score. On stage it is life or death, and some very essential parts of you may surface which go beyond the logical, cerebral functions. Only on stage, during high tension, can one find his own truth if one knows how to listen for it. (Ibid.: 323)

Thus, the ability to react to continuously changing circumstances is recognized as vital not only to ensemble performance, but performance in general.

The paradigm of inter-reaction may also be applied to situations where one musician assumes a leadership position. Analysis of the following rehearsal excerpt recalls the discussion of leadership by example found in Chapter 2, demonstrating this process and its effects on the rest of the ensemble. Partway through the third movement of Barber's *String Quartet*, the violins play an accompanimental *ostinato* figure. While the cello underpins the ensemble, the viola assumes an expressive melodic line (see Example 5.2 for the corresponding excerpt from the score).

Starting from a *Più tranquillo* marking two bars before the excerpt, the tempo of the excerpt slows at the *tranquillo* marking in bar 41 and a subsequent *allargando sempre* indicated in bar 42. On the first day this movement was rehearsed, the transitions between tempi had not been firmly established. Video Example 5.2 provides a classic example of how an ensemble's shared interpretation of tempo may be motivated directly by a single musician's performance. At the beginning of the video, the violins play their accompanimental figure; whilst not completely

Example 5.2 Samuel Barber, *String Quartet No. 1, Op. 11*. Movement III, bars 39–46

together, the tempo is fairly consistent. At the end of bar 40, the violins relax their crotchets in preparation for the viola's entry at *tranquillo*. However, as the violist begins it becomes apparent that her interpretation of the tempo is significantly slower. Prior to this play-through of the excerpt, the quartet had established that the viola line was most important in this new section, supporting the assumption that the violist would exercise a music-dependent form of leadership. In addition, the violist had previously indicated to the other musicians that her line had to be played below a certain tempo in order to make melodic sense (see Video Example 2.1, first discussed in Chapter 2). By bar 43, the violins and cello have slowed to match the violist's interpretation. More striking, however, is the expressive time taken at the end of bar 45. After misgauging the tempo best suited for the viola, the rest of the quartet appears to pay particularly close attention to her performance for the remainder of her melody. This creates a context within which they can sensitively perform a brief pause between bars 45 and 46.

Analysing this performance in terms of inter-reaction provides a means of understanding how rhythmic disjunction may resolve into a synchronized performance within five bars. Through her performance, the violist asserts her interpretation of how fast the passage should be. This interpretation is transmitted through both aural and visual channels to her fellow performers. Inference, in this context, is not only the presumption of a certain tempo by the way the violist performed, but also recognition of the way the violist has played her melody over time. After the initial minim in the viola line, the last quaver of bar 37 provides the rhythmic information necessary to deduce a tempo. Similarly, the inference stage could also include the quartet members remembering the discussions of tempo that had taken place before this play-through. The varying amounts and kinds of inference occurring around the quartet allow for attunement. In this circumstance, it could be argued that the violist did considerably less attuning than her fellow musicians. However, this is not necessarily negative; simply, the manner in which she played her melodic line is recognized by her peers to be most appropriate in this situation. As this example demonstrates, group performance allows for efficient resolution of interpretative differences amongst the quartet, enabling them to share common musical intentions.

This video example demonstrates how musical leadership by example may be directly observed. I would argue that the violist was not explicitly 'communicating' her interpretation to the other quartet members. However, she performs in a specific style and tempo whilst deliberately *not* attuning. In doing so, she forcefully shifts the ensemble's shared interpretation of tempo within this excerpt. Contrary to her normally responsive playing style, the violist's inflexibility in tempo in this context suggests that she is interpretatively controlling this part of the piece. Thus, leadership by example may be interpreted as a playing approach that emphasizes attunement less than interpretative authority.[13]

The final example provides an instance where a performer explicitly cues other musicians within an ensemble. In the first movement of Barber's *String Quartet*, there is a gradual slowing of tempo during a transition before a new thematic idea. The primary feature of this excerpt is a small, three-note motive that is passed around the quartet, finally ending up in the cello part (see Example 5.3 for the corresponding excerpt from the score).

The tempo of this excerpt gradually slows down, only to be restored within a matter of beats. A *rallentando molto* is marked in bar 36, slowing the ensemble from its prior *tranquillo* expressive indication. At the introduction of the new theme

---

[13] This is not to say that leadership by example is always beneficial to ensemble performance. If the violist was repeatedly insistent on her own interpretation, she may not be perceived as a terribly good chamber musician, regardless of her technical prowess. Chapter 6 includes further discussion of how musicians' social or performative qualities may be perceived within ensembles.

Example 5.3   Samuel Barber, *String Quartet No. 1, Op. 11*. Movement I, bars 35–38

on the third beat of bar 37, the tempo is picked up again. Observation of the Boult Quartet in rehearsal reveals that ownership of the transition from the *rallentando molto* to the *a tempo* is passed to the person who has the last moving line before the new theme. Thus, whilst the moving line is handed off between performers, the cellist controls the final stages of the *rallentando*. In Video Example 5.3, the cellist slowly nods after playing the final appearance of the three-note motive, a gesture clearly observed by the violinists. Subsequently, the quartet can cohesively perform the remainder of bar 37.

In this circumstance, the cellist's nod is not directly tied to a sound-producing or sound-accompanying gesture and serves as a form of intentional communication. Through their recognition of the nod as a structural indicator,[14] the other quartet members attribute meaning to the conducted gesture; regardless of its intention, the nod acts as communication. Viewed in relation to inter-reaction, the visual information provided by the cellist's nod is first transmitted to the rest of the ensemble. Upon receiving this information, the other musicians infer intention and meaning to the gesture. It is important to note that the quartet members distinguish this gesture from other physical movements due to their experiences seeing communicative gestures like this used by fellow musicians and conductors. This allows them to deduce that the gesture is intended to communicate both temporal and expressive qualities: the timing of the nod and the manner in

---

[14]   Jane Ginsborg et al. explore how shared performance cues such as that demonstrated by the cellist may serve as effective tools or landmarks within a piece (2006). Their research focuses on how these cues may provide the necessary impetus to 'provide the retrieval cues to activate [an] upcoming passage in long-term memory' (Ibid.: 189). The role memory plays within ensemble performance, particularly when considered in terms of embodied knowledge, may prove to be a fruitful extension of this research.

which it is executed may be 'read' into to varying degrees. From there, the other musicians can consolidate common intentions regarding the timing of the excerpt and subsequently modify their performance. This enables the quartet to navigate through and perform effectively what may otherwise have been a difficult transition for an unconducted ensemble. In this way, inter-reaction accounts for situations of explicit communication between coperformers. However, as has been demonstrated throughout this text, these situations comprise only one aspect of the variety of processes that occur within ensembles.

Conclusion

Through the development of concepts such as shared and attributed intention, the inference of musical intentions, and attunement, this chapter has provided a platform upon which I have proposed a new paradigm for understanding ensemble interaction. Inter-reaction is based upon three steps: transmitting, inferring and attuning. Individual musicians' performances within ensembles are transmitted multimodally to their fellow ensemble members. This sensory media may be regarded as meaningful to those who have sufficient experience with that specific form of instrumental performance. Upon receiving this information, ensemble members can infer the performer's musical intentions (or the results of accidental actions) based upon the embodied environmental knowledge they have accumulated through experience as performers and listeners. The ensemble musicians then apply the inferred musical interpretation and their colleague's impending performance to their own intentions, constantly modifying and shifting their concurrent performances. As each musician's performance unfolds, both it and the actions required to produce it affect the ways the rest of the ensemble's performance evolves. This framework therefore allows for the creative flexibility and spontaneity that is often prized within ensemble performance in Western art music without rejecting the possibility of explicit communication between coperformers.

The examples of ensemble interaction provided in this chapter illustrate the range of experiences that may be accounted for through application of the framework of inter-reaction. First, it may be used to explain how musicians transmit qualitative musical information to their coperformers without explicit communication. In such a manner, ensemble musicians effectively 'pull' information from each other's unfolding performances. Second, the framework provides a model by which musical leadership through example may be exercised. In this way, a single performer can influence the ensemble's shared musical intentions without 'conducting' the group or requiring direct communication. Third, the framework allows explicit communication to exist as a distinct species of interaction within ensembles. Performers within ensembles *do* communicate with each other through gestural cues and eye contact, but this form of communication is only one aspect of ensemble interaction.

The final chapter of this book looks beyond ensemble interaction, exploring the extent to which this framework may inform both musicological and non-musicological research. In addition, it will allow for a critique of the methodologies used within this project, particularly with regard to the application of reflective practice to performance studies. From these topics, however, remains the overarching question of identifying a musical epistemology based not in propositional knowledge, but in performance. Whilst admittedly too large a question to be effectively approached within this book, the possibility remains that musical performance engages with the human mind so as to develop and employ a form of embodied knowledge distinct from other intellectual pursuits.

Chapter 6
Reflecting on Musical Knowledge

Musical ensembles provide instances of human interaction that involve 'a degree of intimacy and subtlety possibly not equalled by any other kind of group' (Young and Colman, 1979: 12) – characteristics that have become increasingly apparent throughout this text. Accordingly, research into the inner, mechanical workings of ensembles requires an investigative perspective that accounts for the unique nature of human interaction they engender. This entails a multidisciplinary approach to fields drawn upon and methodologies used. Preparation of this book has used an amalgamated research method based upon action research. Within this structure, I have applied practice-based and academic methods, drawing upon musicological, sociological and psychological research. My work has led to a critique of not only current frameworks of ensemble interaction, but also the fundamental assumptions upon which they are based. Through this critique, I propose a new framework for understanding ensemble interaction based upon inter-reaction. This framework provides a method by which the interrelationships found within an ensemble may be understood in a way not dependent on the paradigm of communication.

In the final chapter of this book I extend the reflective process embedded in my methodology in three contrasting directions. First, I will reflect upon the research that I have drawn upon over the course of my doctorate (and, in effect, as long as I have been learning about music). This consists of an evaluation of how the work presented within this book may be effectively applied to other research in musicology, gestural studies, pedagogy, epistemology and management studies. Second, I will reflect upon the process of researching and writing this book. Reflective practice is still gaining traction within the performance research community, particularly in academic contexts. I hope that critical self-appraisal of the methods (and the methodological ideals) used within my research will encourage others to further develop this approach. Third, I will speculate on the implications my research may have on philosophical questions of musical knowledge. It has become increasingly apparent that there are many ways that musical thought may be identified, with embodied performative knowledge being only one aspect. Applying the concept of Mode 2 knowledge to musical performance has led to the prospect that musicians may think *through* music as much as or more than they may think *about* music. This proposal prompts a discussion of the nature of musical epistemology, a field of music philosophy that may be more practical than abstract.

Reflecting on Research

As demonstrated in the previous chapter, the framework of inter-reaction, along with conclusions made throughout this text, provides one method of understanding the processes within ensemble performance. However, the discussions that have taken place in constructing this analytical framework may also provide insight into other areas. This section of the chapter will explore ways in which these discussions and the resultant framework may impact further research in musicology and elsewhere. Given the exploratory nature of these discussions, there will be many open-ended questions which will hopefully provide starting points for further academic and practice-led investigations.

The first extension of my research explores the extent to which inter-reaction may apply to improvisatory ensembles, looking beyond the attunement of interpretations to the attunement of larger musical ideas. The second proposed extension moves beyond using the framework as an analytical tool, instead considering how inter-reaction may increase understanding of practitioner concepts of musicality. After exploring these two musicological areas, this section will conclude with a discussion on how my research, informed by various non-musicological fields, may reflect back upon similar research in those fields. Acknowledging that I am not a management theorist, sociologist or psychologist, I hope that this portion of the chapter will prove useful to interdisciplinary researchers interested in nonlinguistic social interaction.

Beyond Interpretation to Creation

The rehearsal excerpts analysed in the previous chapter demonstrate how inter-reaction may be applied to situations where an ensemble shares the creation of interpretation from a written score. It may be possible, however, to extend the applicability of this framework beyond the modification of interpretation to broader concerns of improvisatory musical creation itself. To explore this proposal, it is necessary to apply inter-reaction to contexts where there is no score. Through this, the interplay of emergent musical elements and interpretations may be observed.

Improvised ensembles may provide a more direct means by which non-performing observers can see the impact of musicians' interpretations on subsequent musical events. Within improvised contexts, the malleable nature of interpretation is extended to the music's pitches, rhythms and textures.[1] Causal effects between musical interpretations may therefore be more evident to observers. The following examples, drawn from an improvised performance setting, are distinctly less

---

[1]   To clarify, the improvised contexts to which I refer are those which have no set parts, score or harmonic structure. There may be, however, a rough shape planned for the performance such as 'Start loud, then progressively get softer over the course of ten minutes'. It is possible (and probable) that inter-reaction takes place within partially improvised ensembles who play from a lead sheet.

subtle than the examples of notated Western classical music. In addition to the observational research I conducted at Birmingham Conservatoire, I participated in a variety of ensembles, not the least of which was The Supergroup. Playing entirely improvised music, the group comprised five doctoral candidates at the Conservatoire: Seán Clancy on alto saxophone and melodica, Roberto Alonso Trillo on violin, Sebastiano Dessanay on double bass, Tychonas Michailidis on live electronics and myself on bass trombone. Seán, Sebastiano and Tychonas are composers and performers, whilst Roberto and I focus on musicological research. Beyond agreeing on the general shape of the piece before the concert, the content of each piece was improvised, allowing us to explore interpretative tendencies through performance.

This section briefly examines two excerpts of a performance by The Supergroup in order to gauge the validity of inter-reaction to describe processes occurring in improvised ensemble settings.[2] Video Example 6.1 begins with Sebastiano rhythmically striking the front of his bass with two hands, Roberto playing *altissimo* long notes, Seán holding softer tone clusters in the background on the melodica and Tychonas providing underlying dense electronic textures. As the piece progresses, Roberto begins to play aggressive, double-stopped interjections. Within a matter of seconds, Sebastiano abandons his percussive ostinato to trade double-stopped outbursts with Roberto. Meanwhile, I start playing a muted rhythmic line. Whilst not as active as the one previously played by Sebastiano, it provides a strict pattern against which other lines contrast. Through the framework of inter-reaction, it is possible to see how quickly the musical landscape evolves due to the performances taking place. Upon Roberto's departure from his previous musical line, he introduces a new texture to the ensemble. The rest of the group perceive his performance and alter both their shared musical intentions and their concurrent performances to varying degrees. Sebastiano makes the most distinct change by imitating Roberto's textures in counterpoint. The disappearance of the rhythmic ostinato encourages me to assume that musical role – not mimicking it, but fulfilling its general characteristics. In this way, transmitting, inferring and attuning are evident in a brief improvised interchange.

The second video example comes from later in the same performance. In Video Example 6.2, we can see how one distinct musical element may change the course of a piece. At this point in the performance, the musical texture has become increasingly busy and loud. Seán's outbursts on the alto saxophone have emerged from interjections such as those Roberto and Sebastiano played in the previous excerpt. Out of these flurries of notes a sustained *altissimo* line rises, becoming increasingly prominent. As Seán continues his long notes, Roberto plays higher and higher on his violin, eventually arriving within the same octave as Seán. As the momentum of the group eases, Seán and Sebastiano's sounds fade while Roberto begins a downward *glissando*. I start whistling the saxophone pitch, providing an echo of the previously piercing sounds. In this circumstance,

---

[2]   *Improv.*, Birmingham Conservatoire, 19 January 2011: *Waltz of the Tearing Tears.*

inter-reaction may be applied on a larger scale than seen before. Seán's *altissimo* lines were transmitted to the rest of the ensemble primarily through aural means. Due to its persistence, this musical intention was gained importance within the ensemble, enough so that Roberto altered his own musical intention to join in. As the moment passed, I reacted in a different manner. This encouraged the emergence of a new musical element, based on the pitches previously heard and the direction in which the dynamic was heading. At this scale, the framework may allow for analysis of the shared intentions of the ensemble, a proposal that mirrors conversations that occurred in rehearsals of The Supergroup. Both Roberto and Seán comment that it is important to sense the 'direction' the music is going in, texturally, harmonically or expressively. From there, Roberto describes the importance of being 'a part of what's happening; letting the material you have inside come out … in a kind of unconscious way' (Rehearsal 1, 17:03). In this way, the effect of interpretations upon each other may provide insight into how improvised pieces are created out of the myriad of musical intentions that dwell within musicians.

Roberto's use of the word 'unconscious' raises an important question about the actions involved in ensemble performance. For all their fluidity and spontaneity, is it accurate to call the actions used during performance, particularly those involved in inter-reaction, unconscious? Given the discussions that have taken place throughout this text, I propose that these actions may exist between consciousness and unconsciousness. On one hand, the practice of skilled musicians such as Roberto and the rest of The Supergroup relies on a large amount of embodied knowledge. Ensemble performance engages knowledge *through* playing music: knowledge that evades traditional (Mode 1) analysis. This may encourage the feeling that its use is 'unconscious' or 'intuitive'. On the other hand, skilled musical performance entails the automation of many actions and processes. Even the complexities inherent within inter-reaction may become subsumed into the overarching activity of playing music. Hence, performers may be unaware that they are exercising knowledge and succumb to the historical predisposition that knowledge is limited to that which is known propositionally. The distinction between actions automated through embodied knowledge and purely unconscious action becomes apparent when considering what is a conscious action for one person may be unconscious for another. For a non-musician, the enormity of the task of playing correct notes in time, in tune and with a compelling interpretation may be overwhelming. However, the same task in the hands of an experienced musician may appear to be effortless. Even so, the experienced musician is still cognitively involved in performance. It is through the embodiment and automation of many processes that skilled musicians may perform in such a manner. The embodied musical knowledge exercised, as a form of Mode 2 knowledge, circumvents traditional analysis and therefore appears to be unconscious.

Whilst inter-reaction may allow for insight into the ways an improvised performance may develop, it is important to recognize that such analysis cannot (and should not) account for all of the variables at play. The creation of musical intention and interpretation emerges from a host of informants (Hellaby, 2009). In ensemble performance (both improvised and notated), the emergent musical intentions of the other ensemble members may act as another informant. The importance of inter-reaction may vary from group to group, performance to performance and even bar to bar. However, although inter-reaction may not be prominent in a musician's mind at any given time, it underpins group performance. All ensemble interaction, to a certain degree, must involve some element of inter-reaction. Otherwise, the resulting performance would simply be multiple simultaneous solo performances, with the illusion of cohesiveness arising out of coincidental similarities between interpretations.

Redefining Musicality

Beyond its applicability as a means to analyse ensemble interaction, inter-reaction may provide further insight into general musical qualities themselves. Observation of skilled musicians within ensembles, paired with reflection of the processes by which musicians inter-react and assume leadership, allows for an exploration of what it means to be a 'musical' ensemble musician. To call someone musical entails that they embody a certain set of contextual characteristics. Stephen Malloch and Colwyn Trevarthen's edited volume, *Communicative Musicality: Exploring the Basis of Human Companionship* (2008), operates from the premise that musicality is based on the relationships engendered between performer and audience. In this way, to call someone 'musical' is to address their ability to connect with others through music. Musicality in children often refers to a range of qualities, from 'an infant's predisposition towards melodic contour' and participation in 'rhythmic displays' to the emergence of spontaneous songs (Forrester, 2010: 131–2). Likewise, Susan Hallam has found that the identification of general musical ability across all age groups depends on 'having a sense of rhythm' and 'expressing thoughts and feelings through sound' significantly more than the ability to read music or even being knowledgable about music (2010: 314). This use of 'musical' refers to a person's propensity towards music itself. When used amongst people who are already musicians, however, calling them or their performances 'musical' has a different connotation. The term may imply that whilst a musician is not technically proficient, their innate aptitude and expressiveness creates an aesthetically appealing performance. Used in this way, 'musical' may be patronizing: superficially complimentary, yet subtly demeaning. However, it is not always used in a negative manner. Within ensemble contexts, to call someone musical implies that they blend well with other performers, contributing just enough to be creative but not overbearing. The opposite would be to call that person a soloist – someone who may be fully proficient in other areas of performance, but lacking in the abilities necessary to effectively participate within a chamber group. Writing in 1925, but echoing a sentiment widely expressed throughout the musical community even today, Norton writes that:

it is well known that the great violinist is not necessarily a good quartet-player: his individualistic vitality, noble that it may be, disrupts the spirit of ensemble music. Even four equally accomplished virtuosi do not constitute a quartet: the *mere* virtuoso remains hopelessly foreign to the style while he who grasps the musical intention has difficulty in subjecting his habits of individuality to the whole. (1925: 11)

Among musicians, the concept of being musical within ensembles is often considered intangible and mystical, consisting of characteristics that vary from person to person and context to context. Although the specific properties entailed in being musical are enigmatic, however, the word is used commonly without confusion.

The framework of inter-reaction may help provide a functional definition of musicality within ensemble performance. Recalling the innumerable musicians with whom I have had the pleasure of performing, there are many that I would characterize as being easy to play with. Likewise, there are others that are distinctly hard to play with. Recalling Norton's comment about virtuoso performers who are ill-suited for group performance, a musician may play very sensitively or expressively and still not exhibit the characteristics that make them an ideal ensemble member. In consideration of Turino's two forms of live musical performance, these musicians may be viewed as embracing more presentational ideologies than participatory – more focused on music as an object rather than an interpersonal process. Upon reflection, the performers that I would qualify as good ensemble musicians embody many or all of the qualities that are required to inter-react effectively. Using the three stages of the framework as a guide, the following musical characteristics may be proposed.

- *Transmitting*: A musical ensemble performer needs to have a basic amount of instrumental skill and technique. The ability to effectively transmit one's musical intentions through performance is a prerequisite for the other characteristics of being a musical ensemble participant, even if those intentions may not always be grasped by observers. Regardless of their aural acuity, sensitivity or creativity, if musicians are unable to successfully articulate their musical intention, they cannot function within an ensemble (and may therefore be called musical in a slightly negative manner).
- *Inferring*: The ability to accurately and quickly determine others' musical intentions may be considered one form of sensitive playing. The more easily a musician draws musical inferences from their coperformers, the less time the ensemble has to spend engaged in explicit communication. This enables the ensemble to focus on creating interesting and expressive performances than attaining temporal or interpretational cohesiveness.[3]

---

[3]   I do not intend to negatively portray direct communication through this description. As a tool, it serves a valuable purpose in allowing coperformers to express certain kinds

Receptiveness to others' interpretative ideas may therefore be considered an important trait of a musical ensemble performer.

- *Attuning*: Effective attunement combines the skills and abilities discussed in the previous two stages. In order to attune, a performer needs to possess awareness of the shifting conditions within an ensemble and the technical and creative skill required to contribute the ensemble's shared intentions. Additionally, it includes one's potential to lead by example, should it be contextually appropriate. Therefore, to be a musical ensemble performer, one needs to be both receptive and ready to change, with the overarching priority being the creation of mutually shared intentions as well as the achievement of Turino's 'ideal … human relationships' (2008: 19).

The musical abilities outlined above are all vital to being considered a musical ensemble performer. Granted, being musical in this manner is not a quantifiable characteristic, and I would not presume to set such an flexible concept in stone. I hope that this discussion will provide insight into the qualities which may constitute musicality within chamber ensembles, as well as inspire further critical examination of this concept. Through research on this and other concepts held firmly within the parlance of performers, it may be possible to understand more clearly the culture of performance in a way emergent from practice itself.

Beyond Performance Studies

As demonstrated throughout this book, research on musical ensembles draws on a combination of theories and conclusions from musical and nonmusical fields. Up to this point, the methodological slant of this text has been the application of nonmusical research upon musical contexts. In what ways, however, may current musicological performance research inform other fields? The final discussion of this section explores possible ways in which this flow of research may be reversed. From the variety of fields that have proven useful to this research, I will briefly consider four areas that may benefit from reapplication: gestural studies, pedagogy, epistemology and management studies. I would like to stress that my understanding of these fields is through my understanding as a musician turned academic, and would therefore not presume my ideas on these topics to be new or significant. However, a fresh perspective informed by a different realm of practical experience may provide insights that otherwise may be inaccessible.

In Chapter 2, I identified work by David McNeill, Paul Ekman and Wallace Friesen (among others) as the basis for musicological research on gestures in solo performance. Through that chapter, however, it has become apparent that analysis of gestures in this manner relies upon a paradigm of communication. Given the

---

of information efficiently and effectively. However, it constitutes only one element of ensemble interaction and may not be suitable for all kinds of information that may need to be shared between performers.

arguments I have made against the sole use of a communicative paradigm in ensemble analysis, could non-musicological research on gesture be affected by a similar paradigmatic shift? Work conducted Cassell and McNeill has shown that physical gestures that accompany speech can serve multiple purposes, primarily in the form of cognitive aids for the speaker or the receiver (1991). However, the role of inference in inter-reaction may provide insight not only into how people interpret others' movements (particularly in nonlinguistic situations), but also how these processes may contribute to emergent relationships. Recalling that embodied knowledge is built upon experience, personal experience will influence the degree to which someone may effectively 'read' the world around them (Nonaka and von Krogh, 2009). As has been shown in relation to instrumental performance, my experience as a trombonist allows for specific insight into the processes necessary to play the trombone. Likewise, continued exposure to a certain performer will enable me to accrue an understanding of the motions that person uses to create certain musical results. Might this principle be applied back to the realm of nonmusical social interaction? This proposal recalls Runeson and Frykholm's statement that 'person-and-action perception may [require] the utmost of educated attention' (1983: 598). For example, gestural researchers have accumulated a vast amount of embodied knowledge in regard to perceiving and interpreting others' physical motions. Consequently, they are able to read further into what they perceive others to be doing, going as far as McNeill and Duncan's recognition of mental growth points (2000). Alternatively, those lacking experience with social interaction – or, more conceivably, within a culture's idiosyncratic social interaction – will have significantly more difficulty identifying and perceiving specific gestures, let alone attributing meaning to them. This may affect emergent relationships and achievement of Turino's sameness or Turner's communitas. As demonstrated in my research, the role embodied knowledge plays in social inference is by no means negligible. It may be worth, therefore, pursuing further the relationship between embodied knowledge and perception.

As detailed throughout this book, a common theme of research on ensemble interaction is how leadership operates in a musical setting. In Chapter 2 I critiqued the ways in which concepts of leadership have been applied to theories of ensemble interaction. Through the construction of the framework of inter-reaction, I have identified the model of alternating leadership as the most direct correlate to the processes that occur in ensemble musical performance. As we have seen, chamber musicians do 'temporarily and freely' alternate between being observers, followers, and ad hoc leaders to modify the definition of alternating leadership. However, the underlying methods that enable this shifting of group role have not been explicitly determined. The ways in which musicians within chamber ensembles operate, analysed in relation to inter-reaction, may provide insight into how alternating leadership might function in other social situations. In the previous chapter, I noted the importance of shared intentions in terms of the joint creation and maintenance of an ensemble interpretation. The establishment of interpretation through performance is a constant give-and-take; a lack of flexibility on any one musician's part would result in a performance that is either lacklustre or contains only that person's interpretation. The interpretation emergent through performance may not be predetermined by any of the ensemble members, but is an amalgamation of the individual musicians' aesthetic preferences and the contextual conditions of the performance itself. Similarly, alternating leadership may thrive in circumstances where the overarching goals of a group are identifiable, but not tied to any specific method or subsidiary goals. Therefore, when considering the hierarchy of intention identified by Tomasello et al. (2005: 3), combining concrete higher-level intentions and flexible, inter-reactive action plans may encourage the development of alternating leadership. I would presume that such an arrangement has not already been described within business management research. Rather, I propose that musical ensembles exemplify how successfully this leadership arrangement may work. Moreover, I would argue that not only are few ensembles aware of the role shared intentions play in the determination of leadership, but that such Mode 1 knowledge is not necessary for effective collaboration. Thus, chamber ensembles could serve as an effective foil against which leadership models may be compared.

The differences between Mode 1 and Mode 2 knowledge has been stressed throughout this text. This distinction encompasses the unique form each takes in daily life and the differing ways they may fit into pedagogic approaches. Mode 1 knowledge is generally taught due to its ability to be reduced to specific, communicable concepts. Mode 2 knowledge, on the other hand, resists not only reduction but also transference to a mode of experience other than the medium in which it was created. Instrumental pedagogy and individual practice provide examples of the interplay between these two forms of knowledge, as described in Chapter 5. Within this section, I speculate further upon how musicians' acquisition of skills required for proficiency on their instruments may provide insight into the practical nature of these modes of knowledge as well as the development of reflective practice. Reflecting upon my experiences learning to play the trombone, teaching others to play the instrument and teaching others how to teach their own students, the balance between these modes of knowledge constantly shifts throughout the learning process.[4]*In the earliest lessons, the teacher is generally more direct with the student, describing how to hold the instrument, the position of the body and the movements that need to take place: examples of Mode 1 knowledge that can be explicitly verbalized. Guiding the student thus, they also provide positive reinforcement when the student achieves a goal, however small. It follows that, as the student becomes increasingly experienced, they may focus less on technical specifications (that is to say, action plans) and more on executing higher-level intentions. Through this process, the student unconsciously shifts emphasis from Mode 1 to Mode 2 knowledge. Paralleling this shift from one mode

---

[4]   I do not claim to represent the processes by which all or even most instrumental tutors teach. However, I would argue that the following general characteristics may be found throughout the acquisition of taught skills.

of knowledge to the other, students may correspondingly require less time engaged in a propositionally pedagogic relationship with their teacher. Implicit throughout the acquisition of instrumental technique is the art of effective self-reflection. Through critique of the student's performances, the teacher demonstrates the causality inherent in instrumental performance, encouraging the student to 'fix' playing errors on their own. As a student develops, they reflect upon and critique their own performances through individual practice, exhibiting what Argyris and Schön describe as double-loop learning (1996: 21). Kristina Arévalo et al. describe this form of learning as 'not "simply doing things right" but "doing the right things"', thus modifying the ways in which the musician solves a particular performance 'problem' rather than simply applying the techniques that have been propositionally taught to them (2010: 32). The more advanced a performer becomes, the more they may critique not only their own practices, but also the underlying instrumental technique itself, displaying triple-loop learning. This critical thought is a form of meta-reflective practice, which Schön refers to as moving up a 'ladder of reflection' (1987: 114). The lowest rung of the ladder is the activity itself, with each higher rung reflecting on the one immediately prior. Through this process, musicians can teach in a manner that is not simply the repetition of propositional concepts, but emergent from direct, practical experience. The development of musical technique may provide a concrete example of the influence of Mode 1 and Mode 2 knowledge on pedagogy as well as the development of self-reflection. In this manner, the acquisition of instrumental technique may effectively inform educational and epistemological research.

The research in this book would have been impossible if not for the influence of fields outside musicology. No academic field should be insular; conclusions from one area may impact on and be impacted on by numerous others. I propose that performance studies may similarly inform other non-musicological fields, particularly gestural studies, pedagogy and epistemology, and business management. The examples provided in this section are those that may be the most likely starting points for interdisciplinary research; however, I do not intend to limit such speculation. The next section of this chapter will investigate the effectiveness of the methods used within this research, critiquing the amalgam of practitioner and academic techniques proposed in Chapter 1. This discussion extends the topics of this final chapter into the realm of methodology, providing an opportunity to evaluate musical practice as research.

Reflecting on Reflecting

The evolution of this book relied upon the cyclical nature of action research. The process of action and reflection has continually allowed me to critique and alter my own research practices in line with increasingly evident themes and conclusions. However, reflective practice is only now gaining significant traction within musicological research.[5] Therefore, critique of the methodologies used within my doctoral studies may benefit fellow researchers and musicians who are interested in drawing upon action research and reflective practice. Likewise, this will enable me to engage in reflective practice on a larger level than has taken place thus far in the text. This section of the chapter begins with the positive and negative aspects of using reflective practice as the methodological basis for this research project. From there, I will illustrate the impact this ideological decision has had on the conclusions reached as well as the formation of my doctoral research itself. These personal accounts will constitute the background necessary for an evaluation of the efficacy of practice as research within performance studies, musicology and the arts in general.

Critique of Methodology

Throughout this research, I have engaged in reflective practice on multiple levels, ranging from examining the most fundamental processes of playing a note on my bass trombone to considering how I have developed as a musician. The current discussion raises this reflective process to a higher level, assessing the effectiveness of the methods used within my doctoral research. As will become apparent, the decision to structure my work around action research significantly affected both the organization of my research and the conclusions I have reached. Consequently, the way I have approached the research questions in this text will inform the direction I may take in future research. This section will explore the benefits and challenges that may entail an action research examination of musical performance. From this perspective, it will be possible to enlarge the breadth of reflection even further, assessing the role of practice as research within the arts.

Inadvertently, the structure of this book parallels my own interpretative journey throughout my doctorate. Upon beginning, I was enamoured with 'cracking the code' of performers' gestures and identifying specific group roles within ensembles. As I reflected further, deeper issues arose in terms of the underlying assumptions these objectives were based on. This required me to rethink the entire paradigm by which ensemble performance may be understood. From this perspective, I could then build my own framework for how I could logically explain ensemble interaction without reconciling my understanding as a musician. My research path proved to be the most suitable for explaining my conclusions, resulting in the flow of argument found within this book.

My original motivation for applying action research within this project was to circumvent the problematic divide between Mode 1 and Mode 2 knowledge.

---

5   The Centre for Musical Performance as Creative Practice Performance Studies Network International Conferences, held in Cambridge in July 2011, April 2013, and forthcoming in July 2014, provide many examples of practice-led research. However, the majority of musicological conferences taking place within recent history have not featured this methodological approach in such a prominent manner.

Although I had not consolidated my research questions, I knew that my work had to draw heavily on musicians' experiences themselves. A methodological approach such as the one described in Chapter 1 provided access to the practical knowledge required for my work. Beyond this, the application of action research resulted in four distinct benefits. First, I was not only allowed to continue performing through my research, but was actively encouraged to do so. The ability to take part in the musical life at Birmingham Conservatoire, especially during the first two years of my study, proved invaluable to my work. Second, my roles as performer and researcher were a vital element in the development of the argument I present within this book. All of the theoretical work I conducted was constantly validated against and guided by musical experience. Additionally, I applied the practical knowledge I acquired as a musician to effectively critique the research that has been taking place within performance studies. Reflective practice enabled me to perpetually question my rationale until I arrived at conclusions that aligned theoretical understanding with practical experience. Third, the continual adjustment of research based upon prior evidence encouraged a flexible approach to the research process. Conclusions affected the way I progressed topic to topic and influenced what the research questions actually ended up being. For example, categorization of ensemble musicians' gestures became secondary to the root concern of whether performers were actively 'pushing' information to each other. Thus, I adapted my methodological approach while I conducted it, enabling my research to creatively and organically unfold. Fourth, and most importantly, the continuous exposure to performance prevented my research from turning into a nonmusical endeavour. Given that my work relies heavily on the fields of psychology, sociology and business management (among others), I need to resist the tendency as a musicologist to become enamoured with one of these nonmusical areas. Such a shift in focus would result in a psychological or sociological study *on* music, a strategy that will inevitably fall back into Mode 1 knowledge. My musical involvement emphasized that all of the research I conducted, regardless of its source, was tempered and critiqued through my practical knowledge. As Peter Johnson asked me after reviewing a particularly interdisciplinary section of my text, 'Where is the music?' If the conclusions that emerge from my reflective practice cannot be applied back to music, I have conducted propositional research. Brydon-Miller et al. write that 'action research goes beyond the notion that theory can inform practice, to a recognition that theory can and should be generated through practice' (2003: 15). Importantly, though, they continue, 'theory is really only useful insofar as it is put in the service of a practice focused on achieving positive social change' (Ibid.: 15). Therefore, my musical reflective practice should be part of a larger process of action and reflection where conclusions continually inform practice.

Although structuring my doctoral programme around action research yielded significant benefits, this approach proved challenging in one major respect. As positive as it was, the flexibility inherent in reflective practice provided a source of tension. Due to its malleable nature, my overarching plan of research shifted every few months for the first two years. With each realization of a new topic's importance, the focus of the text changed slightly. Consequently, what was originally intended to be an investigation into 'physical gesture as an agent of collaboration and cohesion in small ensembles' (to quote my research proposal) ended up as an exploration of the phenomenology of musical performance, addressing such philosophical topics as the nature of musical knowledge itself. Until I had settled on a stable argument, regular revision prohibited my doctoral programme from falling into discrete stages such as preliminary research, experimentation and writing up. Whilst Brydon-Miller had warned of the occurrence of 'messes' within action research projects, it took a long time to relinquish minute control over the course of my research. Executing my doctoral programme in this manner required a certain amount of trust: trust in my abilities as a reflective practitioner to effectively critique the material I encountered, trust in those advising me to ensure I would not veer too far from rigorous research, and trust in my sensibilities as a musician to accurately judge which concepts were important and which were irrelevant – a trust mirrored in that which is required for ensemble performance.

Given the benefits and challenges that emerged from the methodological decisions I made throughout my doctoral programme, how well did they allow me to address the research questions at hand? As the four primary questions posed throughout this book are all rooted in performance itself, the application of action research within this course of study allowed access to the practical knowledge inherent in skilled music-making. This provided the context necessary to address larger philosophical questions of musical knowledge, a topic often evaded within strictly positivistic methodologies. In addition to the benefits outlined above, this meant that I retained my performer-ness in personal identity, procedural familiarity and intended consequences. Through this approach, I addressed the research questions in a manner that would benefit academics and practitioners. The challenge of having a 'messy' programme provided a tension not related to my ability to address the questions at hand. For all the directorial uncertainty involved in reflective practice, the result was much more comprehensive than I would have anticipated, encouraging me to continue research and teaching in this manner.

Musical Practice as Research

Extending the previous discussion on the benefits and drawbacks that may arise within action research, I propose that the cycle of action and reflection is an inherent part of skilled musical practice.[6] Alongside development of the procedural knowledge essential to instrumental performance, skilled musicians constantly engage in self-reflection. Although the objectives in place for researchers and musicians may be ostensibly different (those participating in action research

---

[6]   Within this context, I use 'practice' to refer to the application of processes involved in performative musicking and 'individual practice' to refer to the activity of acquiring skill on a musical instrument.

aiming to discern knowledge whilst performers are generally aiming to increase their musical skill in some way or another), I would argue that musicians are forever pursuing a specific kind of knowledge through their practice. Recall the model of action research described in Chapter 1:

1. To develop a *plan* of action to improve what is already happening.
2. To *act* to implement the plan.
3. To *observe* the effects of action in the context in which it occurs.
4. To *reflect* on these effects as a basis for further planning, subsequent action and so on, through a succession of cycles.

(Kemmis, 1982: 7; my emphasis)

Innumerable skilled musicians have demonstrated persistent attitudes towards improving themselves and their musical output. This occurs on small and large scales, ranging from individual practice sessions all the way to career-level activities. When applied to musical practice, the steps outlined by Kemmis are neither discrete nor conscious. The practice room provides the most direct example. There, a musician *plans* to fix a technical or expressive problem, which they *enact* by playing through the issue. Subsequently, they *observe* the results of their effort through listening, recording, comparing with a metronome or tuner, or receiving external feedback. Consequently, they *reflect* upon the effectiveness of their endeavour and adjust further plans. This process is not limited to developing technical facilities. Recalling conclusions made throughout this book, learning to play an instrument, learning to be a musician and learning to participate in ensembles develop embodied knowledge. A substantial amount of that knowledge, if not all of it, emerges through musical reflective practice.

Recognizing these similarities, skilled musicians may become involved with musicological research on performance as a natural extension of their own work. Rather than being either subjects to be observed or even partners in research (considering participatory action research), skilled performers may generate their own conclusions regarding questions of performance, interpretation and philosophical topics relating to music. Increased practitioner involvement in performance studies may impact the efficacy of this research in two primary ways. First, comprehensive understanding of topics central to performance studies is only available through the knowledge created by and for practising musicians. These topics include ensemble interaction, the creation of interpretation and a performer's voice, the impact of the audience on performance, among many foreseeable others (including those still to be named). Whilst propositional knowledge may be generated about these areas, they cannot be developed strictly through the use of positivistic methodologies. Second, reflective practitioners will guide researchers to ask the questions most pertinent and critical to practical musical knowledge. Acknowledging longstanding discussions about the relationship between performance and analysis (historical, narratological and theoretical), the analysis in question has historically been limited to knowledge *about* music. Reflective practice provides a window onto knowledge *through* music – the knowledge embedded in performative musicking. Hence, the point of this discussion: musical practice itself is the most fundamental way of interacting with and researching this form of art. Christopher Small writes that music 'is not a thing at all but an activity, something that people do' (1998: 2). Along these lines, I propose that research on music should be intimately tied to making music, not historical research, mathematical analysis, or psychological or narratological profiling. These activities may provide peripheral insight into the context music may have been written or performed in, the ways sound waves interact, or the ways a listener may attribute meaning. From experience, however, they do not directly change the impact that musicians themselves have on the resulting performance. Whilst propositional analysis may contribute to the creation of an interpretation, individual intuition and expression still provide the grounding of truly creative, personal performances. Therefore, musical reflective practice may achieve further understanding of the nature and beauty of music. This is not to say that all performance research should be conducted through critical reflection; as Lakoff and Johnson remark, 'phenomenological reflection, though valuable in revealing the structure of experience, must be supplemented by empirical research into the cognitive unconscious' (1999: 5). Given the nature of performance studies over the past two decades, however, empirical research vastly outweighs phenomenological reflection – a situation that may be remedied through the involvement of more skilled practitioners into critical reflection.

The final section of this chapter addresses what has become a recurring theme throughout this book: music as a mode of thought. In Chapter 3 I identified that performers constantly apply Mode 2 knowledge within musical practice, simultaneously engaging multiple modes of sensory perception. The exploration of the phenomenology of individual performance in Chapter 4 illustrates both the dynamic relationship performers have with their instruments and the correlation between intention and effect when aurally manifesting musical interpretation. Combined with the discussion of musicians' abilities of inference, I constructed the framework of inter-reaction in Chapter 5. These conclusions suggest that performers actively think *through* music, a conjecture that may be substantiated through musical reflective practice.

Reflecting on Musical Knowledge

Throughout this text, I have presented arguments on a variety of topics related to performance studies and the epistemology of music. Investigation of the use of physical gesture in ensemble interaction has prompted discussions on leadership, communication, intention, inference and the nature of musical knowledge. In the final section of this chapter, I will draw out the primary arguments emergent from these discussions. Out of these arguments, I will briefly explore the implications of proposing music as a form of Mode 2 knowledge in relation to academic, musical and pedagogic practice.

Physical gestures used in musical performance are idiosyncratic and non-semantic. Given that musicians draw inferences from many if not most observable physical motions their peers make in performance, designating the term 'gesture' as a significant physical movement is not practical. A performer's motions deemed significant by one observer may not be by another. Hence, efforts to create typology of physical gestures may inevitably be frustrated by the singular, malleable nature of motions read as gesture, resulting in categories either too general or too specific to be useful to musicians. Similarly, the use of a communicative paradigm for describing how musicians share information presents an incomplete picture of ensemble interaction. Except in the case of explicit cues and other communicative gestures, movements made whilst playing an instrument emerge through the creation of music itself, and reveal information about performers' musical intentions. From these naturally occurring movements, ensemble musicians can 'pull' qualitative information about their colleagues' musical interpretations. Explicit communication ('pushing' information) happens in addition to the inference that is constantly taking place. Upon processing received information, musicians may consciously or automatically adjust their own performances to the interpretations unfolding around them. Ensemble interaction may be understood in terms of performers transmitting qualitative musical information, inferring musical intentions from others' performance and attuning to those intentions: a cohesive framework of processes called inter-reaction.

Analysing ensemble interaction in terms of inter-reaction significantly affects how leadership may be understood to operate in unconducted musical groups. Ensemble members assume leadership based upon constantly changing circumstances and shared musical intentions. Whilst there may be other impetuses to developing leadership, including the charisma and experience of individual performers, the music being played and the performance itself significantly determine who leads an ensemble. This results in a form of context-dependent alternating leadership. Through inter-reaction, individual contributions to the development of the ensemble's shared intentions may become automated to the extent that it feels to the performers as if the music is 'playing itself'. Likewise, this process may encourage the development of social conditions such as sameness or communitas.

This research has required an in-depth investigation of the phenomenology of individual and ensemble performance. Through this analysis, deeper issues of epistemology have emerged. As musical performance is a form of skilled practice, study of it requires involvement in the practice itself. Whilst critical reflection has its limitations, it is a vital element to understanding the processes inherent in musical performance. The depth of musical experience – both in listening and performance – is exhibited through the colourful and detailed verbal, spatial and graphical metaphors used to describe it. For metaphor to operate in such a manner presupposes that music is its own unique realm of experience. When musicians play music, they become immersed in that experience; thus, it is possible to think *through* music. Inter-reaction depends on the active application of embodied musical knowledge, a form of Mode 2 knowledge that may only be referenced in other realms of experience through metaphor.

Andrew Bowie proposes that the early Romantic philosophers were correct in recognizing that music can powerfully affect listeners even when there is no direct linguistic correlate available, preventing them from knowing what it 'means' (2007). Bowie is interested in the way these philosophers conceived of music as a different world: one of profound importance, but not contingent upon the physical world. Thus, rather than his text 'seeing the role of philosophy as being to determine the nature of the object "music"', it 'focuses on the philosophy which is conveyed by music itself', equating musical experience to higher thinking such as philosophy (Ibid.: xi). Arguing that music is a form of philosophy raises a host of questions regarding the properties of philosophic thought; however, had he rephrased his proposal to consider musical engagement as a mode of thinking, he may have been closer to the mark. Participating in musical performance, particularly when creating a performance, engages the mind with musical content that resists translation into other formats. That content exists in a realm of experience all of its own and is the lifeblood of performance. To play music is to *think* through music, to grapple with musical thoughts and create new musical ideas. Playing music within an ensemble allows performers to interact with their fellow musicians in a manner distinct from that found in other social situations: emergent from and immersed in musical thought.

Select Bibliography

Agawu, K. (2009) *Music as Discourse: Semiotic Adventures in Romantic Music.* Oxford: Oxford University Press.

Aiello, R. (1994) 'Music and Language: Parallels and Contrasts' in R. Aiello (ed.) *Musical Perceptions.* Oxford: Oxford University Press, 40–63.

Altenmüller, E., Wiesendanger, M. and Kesselring, J. (eds) (2006) *Music, Motor Control and the Brain.* Oxford: Oxford University Press.

Andert, D., Platt, A. and Alexakis, G. (2011) 'Alternative, Grassroots, and Rogue Leadership: A Case For Alternating Leaders In Organizations'. *Journal of Applied Business Research* 27/2, 53–61.

Arévalo, K.M., Ljung, M. and Sriskandarajah, N. (2010) 'Learning Through Feedback in the Field: Reflective Learning in a NGO in the Peruvian Amazon'. *Action Research* 8/1, 29–51.

Argyris, C. and Schön, D. (1996) *Organizational Learning II: Theory, Method and Practice.* Reading, MA: Addison-Wesley.

Atik, Y. (1994) 'The Conductor and the Orchestra: Interactive Aspects of the Leadership Process'. *Leadership and Organization Development Journal* 15/1, 22–8.

Barber, S. (1939) *String Quartet No. 1, Op. 11.* New York: G. Schirmer, Inc.

Bargreen, M. (1998) 'Tokyo String Quartet: A Disappointing Night', *The Seattle Times* [online], 15 January. Available at http://community.seattletimes.nwsource.com/archive/?date=19980115&slug=2728794 [accessed 26 September 2011].

Barry, N. and Hallam, S. (2002) 'Practice' in R. Parncutt and G. McPherson (eds) *The Science and Psychology of Music Performance.* Oxford: Oxford University Press, 151–65.

Barthes, R. (1977) *Image–Music–Text*, trans. Stephen Heath. London: Fontana Press.

Bayley, A. (ed.) (2009) *Recorded Music: Performance, Culture and Technology.* Cambridge: Cambridge University Press.

Belbin, R.M. (1993) *Team Roles at Work.* Oxford: Butterworth-Heinemann.

Berliner, P. (1994) *Thinking in Jazz: The Infinite Art of Improvisation.* Chicago: University of Chicago Press.

Blank, M. and Davidson, J. (2007) 'An Exploration of the Effects of Musical and Social Factors in Piano Duo Collaborations'. *Psychology of Music* 35/2, 231–48.

Blauert, J. (1983) *Spatial Hearing: The Psychophysics of Human Sound Localization.* Cambridge, MA: MIT Press.

Blum, D. (1987) *The Art of Quartet Playing: The Guarneri Quartet in Conversation with David Blum.* Ithaca: Cornell University Press.

Bowie, A. (2007) *Music, Philosophy, and Modernity.* Cambridge: Cambridge University Press.

Broughton, M. and Stevens, C. (2009) 'Music, Movement and Marimba: An Investigation of the Role of Movement and Gesture in Communicating Musical Expression to an Audience'. *Psychology of Music* 37, 137–53.

Brydon-Miller, M., Greenwood, D. and Maguire, P. (2003) 'Why Action Research?' *Action Research* 1/1, 9–28.

Burns, J. (1978) *Leadership*. New York: Harper & Row.

Cadoz, C. and Wanderley, M. (2000) 'Gesture – Music' in M. Wanderley and M. Battier (eds) *Trends in Gestural Control of Music* [CD ROM]. Paris: IRCAM, 71–93.

Carson, J.B., Tesluk, P.E. and Marrone, J.A. (2007) 'Shared Leadership in Teams: An Investigation of Antecedent Conditions and Performance'. *Academy of Management Journal* 50/5, 1217–34.

Cassell, J. and McNeill, D. (1991) 'Gesture and the Poetics of Prose'. *Poetics Today* 12/3, 375–404.

Clarke, E. (2002) 'Understanding the Psychology of Performance' in J. Rink (ed.) *Musical Performance: A Guide to Understanding*. Cambridge: Cambridge University Press, 59–72.

Clarke, E. and Davidson, J. (1998) 'The Body in Performance' in W. Thomas (ed.) *Composition, Performance, Reception: Studies in the Creative Process of Music*. Aldershot: Ashgate, 74–92.

Cook, N. (2000) 'Theorizing Mixed Media' in D. Greer (ed.) *Musicology and Sister Disciplines: Past, Present, and Future*. Oxford: Oxford University Press, 552–4.

Cross, I. (2005) 'Music and Meaning, Ambiguity, and Evolution' in D. Miell, R.A.R. MacDonald and D.J. Hargreaves (eds) *Musical Communication*. Oxford: Oxford University Press, 27–44.

Csikszentmihalyi, M. (1990) *Flow: The Psychology of Optimal Experience*. New York: Harper and Row.

Dahl, S. (2006) 'Movements and Analysis of Drumming' in E. Altenmüller, M. Wiesendanger, and J. Kesselring (eds) *Music, Motor Control and the Brain*. Oxford: Oxford University Press, 125–38.

Dahl, S., Bevilacqua, F., Bresin, R., Clayton, M., Leante, L., Poggi, I. and Rasimimanana, N. (2010) 'Gestures in Performance' in R.I. Godøy and M. Leman (eds) *Musical Gestures: Sound, Movement, and Meaning*. New York and London: Routledge, 36–68.

Davidson, J. (1993) 'Visual Perception of Performance Manner in the Movements of Solo Musicians'. *Psychology of Music* 21, 103–13.

— (1997) 'The Social in Musical Performance' in D.J. Hargreaves and A.C. North (eds) *The Social Psychology of Music*. Oxford: Oxford University Press, 209–28.

— (2001) 'The Role of the Body in the Production and Perception of Solo Vocal Performance: A Case Study of Annie Lennox'. *Musicæ Scientiæ* 5/2, 235–56.

— (2002) 'Communicating With the Body in Performance' in J. Rink (ed.) *Musical Performance: A Guide to Understanding*. Cambridge: Cambridge University Press, 144–52.

— (2005) 'Bodily Communication in Musical Performance' in D. Miell, R.A.R. MacDonald and D.J. Hargreaves (eds) *Musical Communication*. Oxford: Oxford University Press, 215–38.

— (2006) '"She's the One": Multiple Functions of Body Movement in a Stage Performance by Robbie Williams' in A. Gritten and E. King (eds) *Music and Gesture*. Aldershot: Ashgate, 208–25.

— (2012) 'Bodily Movement and Facial Actions in Expressive Musical Performance by Solo and Duo Instrumentalists: Two Distinctive Case Studies'. *Psychology of Music* 40/5, 595–633.

Davidson, J. and Good, J. (2002) 'Social and Musical Co-ordination Between Members of a String Quartet: An Exploratory Study'. *Psychology of Music* 30/2, 186–201.

Davidson, J. and King, E. (2004) 'Strategies for Ensemble Practice' in A. Williamon (ed.) *Musical Excellence: Strategies and Techniques to Enhance Performance*. Oxford: Oxford University Press, 105–22.

DeChurch, L.A. and Mesmer-Magnus, J.R. (2010) 'The Cognitive Underpinnings of Effective Teamwork: A Meta-Analysis'. *Journal of Applied Psychology* 95/1, 32–53.

Dewey, J. (1934) *Art as Experience*. New York: Perigree.

Dogantan-Dack, M. (2006) 'The Body Behind Music: Precedents and Prospects'. *Psychology of Music* 34, 449–64.

Douglas, T. (1978) *Basic Groupwork*. London: Routledge.

Dubal, D. (1985) *The World of the Concert Pianist*. London: Gollancz.

Ekman, P. and Friesen, W. (1969) 'The Repertory of Nonverbal Behaviour: Categories, Origins, Usage and Coding'. *Semiotica* 1, 49–98.

Elsdon, P. (2006) 'Listening in the Gaze: The Body in Keith Jarrett's Solo Piano Improvisations' in A. Gritten and E. King (eds) *Music and Gesture*. Aldershot: Ashgate, 192–207.

Elsner, B. and Hommel, B. (2001) 'Effect Anticipation and Action Control'. *Journal of Experimental Psychology: Human Perception and Performance* 27/1, 229–40.

Felfe, J., Tartler, K. and Liepmann, D. (2004) 'Advanced Research in the Field of Transformational Leadership'. *Zeitschrift für Personalforschung* 18/3, 262–88.

Fish, S. (1989) *Doing What Comes Naturally: Change, Rhetoric, and the Practice of Theory in Literary and Legal Studies*. Oxford: Clarendon Press.

Ford, L. and Davidson, J. (2003) 'An Investigation of Members' Roles in Wind Quintets'. *Psychology of Music* 31/1, 53–74.

Forrester, M.A. (2010) 'Emerging Musicality During the Pre-School Years: A Case Study of One Child'. *Psychology of Music* 38/2, 131–58.

Garnett, L. (2009) *Choral Conducting and the Construction of Meaning: Gesture, Voice, Identity*. Farnham: Ashgate.

— (2010) 'Monkey Hear …' in *Helping You Harmonise*. Available at http://www. HelpingYouHarmonise.com/monkeyhear [accessed 4 July 2011].

Gaunt, H. (2007) 'Learning and Teaching Breathing and Oboe Playing: Action Research in a Conservatoire'. *British Journal of Music Education* 24/2, 207–31.

Gilbert, M. (1989) *On Social Facts*. New York: Routledge.

Gilboa, A. and Tal-Shmotkin, M. (2012) 'String Quartets as Self-Managed Teams: An Interdisciplinary Perspective'. *Psychology of Music* 40/1, 19–41.

Gingras, B., Lagrandeur-Ponce, T., Giordano, B.L. and McAdams, S. (2008) 'Effect of Expressive Intent, Performer Expertise, and Listener Expertise on the Perception of Artistic Individuality in Organ Performance' in K. Miyazaki, M. Adachi, Y. Hiraga et al. (eds) *Proceedings of the 10th International Conference on Music Perception and Cognition (ICMPC2008)*. Sapporo, Japan, 10–14.

Ginsborg, J., Chaffin, R. and Nicholson, G. (2006) 'Shared Performance Cues in Singing and Conducting: A Content Analysis of Talk During Practice'. *Psychology of Music* 34, 167–94.

Godøy, R.I. (2010) 'Gestural Affordances of Musical Sound' in R.I. Godøy and M. Leman (eds) *Musical Gestures: Sound, Movement, and Meaning*. New York and London: Routledge, 103–25.

Godøy, R.I. and Leman, M. (eds) (2010) *Musical Gestures: Sound, Movement, and Meaning*. New York and London: Routledge.

Goodman, E. (2002) 'Ensemble Performance' in J. Rink (ed.) *Musical Performance: A Guide to Understanding*. Cambridge: Cambridge University Press, 153–67.

Gritten, A. and King, E. (2011) 'Introduction' in A. Gritten and E. King (eds) *New Perspectives on Music and Gesture*. Farnham: Ashgate, 1–9.

Hallam, S. (2010) '21st Century Conceptions of Musical Ability'. *Psychology of Music* 38/3, 308–30.

Halmrast, T., Guettler, K., Bader, R. and Godøy, R.I. (2010) 'Gesture and Timbre' in R.I. Godøy and M. Leman (eds) *Musical Gestures: Sound, Movement, and Meaning*. New York and London: Routledge, 183–211.

Harris, M. (1976) 'History and Significance of the Emic/Etic Distinction'. *Annual Review of Anthropology* 5, 329–50.

Hatten, R. (2006) 'A Theory of Musical Gesture and its Application to Beethoven and Schubert' in A. Gritten and E. King (eds) *Music and Gesture*. Aldershot: Ashgate, 1–23.

Hellaby, J. (2009) *Reading Musical Interpretation: Case Studies in Solo Piano Performance*. Farnham: Ashgate.

Heron, J. (1999) *The Complete Facilitator's Handbook*. London: Kogan Page.

Herr, K.G. and Anderson, G.L. (2005) *The Action Research Dissertation: A Guide for Students and Faculty*. London: Sage.

Hindriks, F. (2008) 'Intentional Action and the Praise-Blame Asymmetry'. *Philosophical Quarterly* 58/233, 630–41.

Hoffmann, J., Stroecker, C. and Kunde, W. (2004) 'Anticipatory Control of Actions'. *International Journal of Sport & Exercise Psychology* 2/4, 346–61.

Huang, H.B. (2010) 'What is Good Action Research?: Why the Resurgent Interest?' *Action Research* 8/1, 93–109.

Jäncke, L. (2006) 'From Cognition to Action' in E. Altenmüller, M. Wiesendanger and J. Kesselring (eds) *Music, Motor Control and the Brain*. Oxford: Oxford University Press, 25–38.

Jensenius, A.R., Wanderley, M., Godøy, R.I. and Leman, M. (2010) 'Musical Gestures: Concepts and Methods in Research' in R.I. Godøy and M. Leman (eds) *Musical Gestures: Sound, Movement, and Meaning*. New York and London: Routledge, 12–35.

Jerde, T.E., Santello, M., Flanders, M. and Soechting, J.F. (2006) 'Hand Movements and Musical Performance' in E. Altenmüller, M. Wiesendanger, and J. Kesselring (eds) *Music, Motor Control and the Brain*. Oxford: Oxford University Press, 79–90.

Johnson, P. (2002) 'The Legacy of Recordings' in J. Rink (ed.) *Musical Performance: A Guide to Understanding*. Cambridge: Cambridge University Press, 197–212.

Jones, S., Abbott, D. and Ross, S. (2009) 'Redefining the Performing Arts Archive'. *Archival Science* 9/3–4, 165–71.

Kaastra, L. (2008) *Systematic Approaches to the Study of Cognition in Western Art Music Performance*. PhD. University of British Columbia.

Keller, P. and Koch, I. (2008) 'Action Planning in Sequential Skills: Relations to Music Performance'. *The Quarterly Journal of Experimental Psychology* 61/2, 275–91.

Kemmis, S. (ed.) (1982) *The Action Research Reader*. Geelong, Victoria, Australia: Deakin University Press.

King, E. (2006a) 'Supporting Gestures: Breathing in Piano Performance' in A. Gritten and E. King (eds) *Music and Gesture*. Aldershot: Ashgate, 142–64.

— (2006b) 'The Roles of Student Musicians in Quartet Rehearsals'. *Psychology of Music* 34/2, 262–83.

King, E. and Ginsborg, J. (2011) 'Gestures and Glances: Interactions in Ensemble Practice' in A. Gritten and E. King (eds) *New Perspectives on Music and Gesture*. Farnham: Ashgate, 177–201.

Kivy, P. (1995) *Authenticities: Philosophical Reflections on Musical Performance*. Cornell: Cornell University Press.

— (2003) 'Jokes Are a Laughing Matter'. *The Journal of Aesthetics and Art Criticism* 61/1, 5–15.

— (2007) *Music, Language, and Cognition: And Other Essays in the Philosophy of Music*. Oxford: Oxford University Press.

Kleinhammer, E. (1963) *The Art of Trombone Playing*. Los Angeles: Alfred Publishing.

Knobe, J. (2004) 'Intention, Intentional Action and Moral Considerations'. *Analysis* 64, 181–7.

— (2006) 'The Concept of Intentional Action: A Case Study in the Uses of Folk Psychology'. *Philosophical Studies* 130, 203–31.

Kokotsaki, D. (2007) 'Understanding the Ensemble Pianist: A Theoretical Framework'. *Psychology of Music* 35, 641–65.

Kozlowski, S.W.J. and Ilgen, D.R. (2006) 'Enhancing the Effectiveness of Work Groups and Teams'. *Psychological Science in the Public Interest* 7, 77–124.

Kugler, P.N. and Turvey, M.T. (1979) 'Two Metaphors for Neural Afference and Efference'. *Behavioral and Brain Sciences* 2, 305–12.

Kühl, O. (2011) 'The Semiotic Gesture' in A. Gritten and E. King (eds) *New Perspectives on Music and Gesture*. Farnham: Ashgate, 123–9.

Kunde, W., Koch, I. and Hoffmann, J. (2004) 'Anticipated Action Effects Affect the Selection, Initiation, and Execution of Actions'. *Quarterly Journal of Experimental Psychology* 57A/1, 87–106.

Lakoff, G. and Johnson, M. (1980) *Metaphors We Live By*. Chicago: University of Chicago Press.

— (1999) *Philosophy in the Flesh: The Embodied Mind and Its Challenge to Western Thought*. New York: Basic Books.

Leman, M. (2010) 'Music, Gesture, and the Formation of Embodied Meaning' in R.I. Godøy and M. Leman (eds) *Musical Gestures: Sound, Movement, and Meaning*. New York and London: Routledge, 126–53.

Leman, M. and Godøy, R. I. (2010) 'Why Study Musical Gestures?' in R. I. Godøy and M. Leman (eds) *Musical Gestures: Sound, Movement, and Meaning*. New York and London: Routledge, 3–11.

Lerdahl, F. and Jackendoff, R. (1983) *A Generative Theory of Tonal Music*. Cambridge, MA: MIT Press.

McNeill, D. (2000) *Language and Gesture*. Cambridge: Cambridge University Press.

— (2005) *Gesture and Thought*. Chicago: Chicago University Press.

McNeill, D. and Duncan, S.D. (2000) 'Growth Points in Thinking-for-Speaking' in D. McNeill (ed.) *Language and Gesture*. Cambridge: Cambridge University Press, 141–61.

Malloch, S. and Trevarthen, C. (2008) *Communicative Musicality: Exploring the Basis of Human Companionship*. Oxford: Oxford University Press.

Manduell, M. and Wing, A.M. (2007) 'The Dynamics of Ensemble: The Case for Flamenco'. *Psychology of Music* 35/4, 591–627.

Merleau-Ponty, M. (2002) *Phenomenology of Perception*, trans. C. Smith. London: Routledge. (Originally published in 1945.)

Meyer, L. (1994) 'Emotion and Meaning in Music' in R. Aiello (ed.) *Musical Perceptions*. Oxford: Oxford University Press, 3–39.

Michailidis, T. and Bullock, J. (2011) 'Improving Performers' Musicality Through Live Interaction with Haptic Feedback: A Case Study' in S. Zanolla, F. Avanzini, S. Canazza and A. de Götzen (eds) *Proceedings of SMC 2011 8th Sound and Music Computing Conference 'Creativity Rethinks Science'*. Padova, Italy: Padova University Press, 227–32.

Murnighan, J.K. and Conlon, D.E. (1991) 'The Dynamics of Intense Work Groups: A Study of British String Quartets'. *Administrative Science Quarterly* June, 165–86.

Nirkko, A. and Kristeva, R. (2006) 'Brain Activation During String Playing' in E. Altenmüller, M. Wiesendanger and J. Kesselring (eds) *Music, Motor Control and the Brain*. Oxford: Oxford University Press, 189–204.

Nonaka, I. and von Krogh, G. (2009) 'Tacit Knowledge and Knowledge Conversion: Controversy and Advancement in Organizational Knowledge Creation Theory'. *Organization Science* 20/3, 635–52.

Norton, M.D.H. (1925) *String Quartet Playing: A New Treatise on Chamber Music, Its Technic and Interpretation*. New York: Carl Fischer.

Palmer, C. (2006) 'The Nature of Memory for Music Performance Skills' in E. Altenmüller, M. Wiesendanger and J. Kesselring (eds) *Music, Motor Control and the Brain*. Oxford: Oxford University Press, 39–54.

Pecenka, N. and Keller, P. (2009) 'Auditory Pitch Imagery and Its Relationship to Musical Synchronization'. *The Neurosciences and Music III: Disorders and Plasticity (Annals of the New York Academy of Sciences)* 1169, 282–6.

Powers, W. (1974) *Behavior: The Control of Perception*. London: Wildwood House.

Rasch, R.A. (1979) 'Synchronization in Performed Ensemble Music'. *Acoustica* 43, 121–31.

— (1988) 'Timing and Synchronisation in Ensemble Performance' in J.A. Sloboda (ed.) *Generative Processes in Music: The Psychology of Performance, Improvisation, and Composition*. Oxford: Clarendon Press, 70–90.

Rebelo, P. (2010) 'Notating the Unpredictable'. *Contemporary Music Review* 29, 17–27.

Rooley, A. (1990) *Performance: Revealing the Orpheus Within*. Shaftesbury, Dorset: Element Books.

Runeson, S. (1977) *On Visual Perception of Dynamic Events*. PhD dissertation, University of Uppsala, Sweden

Runeson, S. and Frykholm, G. (1981) 'Visual Perception of Lifted Weight'. *Journal of Experimental Psychology: Human Perception and Performance* 7, 733–40.

— (1983) 'Kinematic Specification of Dynamics as an Informational Basis for Person-and-action Perception: Expectations, Recognition and Deceptive Intention'. *Journal of Experimental Psychology: General* 112, 585–615.

Ryle, G. (1949) *The Concept of Mind*. New York: Barnes and Noble.

Saslaw, J. (1996) 'Forces, Containers, and Paths: The Role of Body-Derived Image Schemas in the Conceptualization of Music'. *Journal of Music Theory* 40/2, 217–43.

Sawyer, R.K. (2005) 'Music and Conversation' in D. Miell, R.A.R. MacDonald and D.J. Hargreaves (eds) *Musical Communication*. Oxford: Oxford University Press, 45–60.

Schack, T. and Tenenbaum, G. (2004) 'Effect Representation and Action Planning: A Preface'. *International Journal of Sport and Exercise Psychology* 2/4, 343–5.

Schneider, A. (2010) 'Music and Gestures: A Historical Introduction and Survey of Earlier Research' in R.I. Godøy and M. Leman (eds) *Musical Gestures: Sound, Movement, and Meaning*. New York and London: Routledge, 69–100.

Schön, D. (1983) *The Reflective Practitioner: How Professionals Think in Action.*
    New York: Basic Books.
— (1987) *Educating the Reflective Practitioner.* San Francisco: Jossey-Bass.
Searle, J. (1995) *The Construction of Social Reality.* London: Allen Lane.
Seddon, F. (2005) 'Modes of Communication During Jazz Improvisation'. *British
    Journal of Music Education* 22/1, 47–61.
Seddon, F. and Biasutti, M. (2009) 'A Comparison of Modes of Communication
    Between Members of a String Quartet and a Jazz Sextet'. *Psychology of Music*
    37/4, 395–415.
Shuter-Dyson, R. and Gabriel, C. (eds) (1981) *The Psychology of Musical Ability.*
    London: Methuen.
Sloboda, J. (1985) *The Musical Mind: The Cognitive Psychology of Music.* Oxford:
    Oxford University Press.
Small, C. (1998) *Musicking: The Meanings of Performing and Listening.* Hanover:
    Wesleyan University Press.
Smith, S. and Smith, S. (1981) 'Visual Music'. *Perspectives of New Music* 20/1, 75–93.
Snell, H. (1997) *The Trumpet: Its Practice and Performance, A Guide for Students.*
    Staffordshire: Rakeway Music.
Tomasello, M., Carpenter, M., Call, J., Behne, T. and Moll, H. (2005)
    'Understanding and Sharing Intentions: The Origins of Cultural Cognition'.
    Behavioral and Brain Sciences 28, 1–17.
Tovstiga, G., Odenthal, S. and Goerner, S. (2004) 'Sense-Making and Learning
    in Complex Organizations: The String Quartet Revisited'. Paper presented at
    the Fifth European Conference on Organizational Knowledge, Learning and
    Capabilities, April 2004, Innsbruck.
Trevarthen, C., Delafield-Butt, J. and Schögler, B. (2011) 'Psychobiology of
    Musical Gesture: Innate Rhythm, Harmony and Melody in Movements of
    Narration' in A. Gritten and E. King (eds) *New Perspectives on Music and
    Gesture.* Farnham: Ashgate, 11–43.
Tuomela, R. (1995) *The Importance of Us: A Philosophical Study of Basic Social
    Notion.* Stanford, CA: Stanford University Press.
Turino, T. (2008) *Music as Social Life: The Politics of Participation.* Chicago and
    London: The University of Chicago Press.
Turner, V. (1969) *The Ritual Process.* Chicago: Aldine.
Vines, B., Krumhansl, C., Wanderley, M., Dalca, I. and Levitin, D. (2005)
    'Dimensions of Emotion in Expressive Musical Performance'. *Annals of the
    New York Academy of Sciences* 1060, 1–5.
Wanderley, M. and Vines, B. (2006) 'Origins and Functions of Clarinettists'
    Ancillary Gestures' in A. Gritten and E. King (eds) *Music and Gesture.*
    Aldershot: Ashgate, 165–91.
Whitener, S. (1997) *A Complete Guide to Brass.* Belmont, CA: Schirmer Books.
Wiesendanger, M., Baader, A. and Kazennikov, O. (2006) 'Fingering and Bowing
    in Violinists: A Motor Control Approach' in E. Altenmüller, M. Wiesendanger

and J. Kesselring (eds) *Music, Motor Control and the Brain*. Oxford: Oxford University Press, 109–24.

Williamon, A. and Davidson, J. (2002) 'Exploring Co-Performer Communication'. *Musicæ Scientiæ* 6/1, 53–72.

Wilson, G. and MacDonald, R. (2012) 'The Sign of Silence: Negotiating Musical Identities in an Improvising Ensemble'. *Psychology of Music* 40/5, 558–73.

Windsor, W.L. (2011) 'Gestures in Music-making: Action, Information and Perception' in A. Gritten and E. King (eds) *New Perspectives on Music and Gesture*. Farnham: Ashgate, 45–66.

Young, V.M. and Colman, A.M. (1979) 'Some Psychological Processes in String Quartets'. *Psychology of Music* 7, 12–18.

Zatorre, R.J., Chen, J.L. and Penhune, V.B. (2007) 'When the Brain Plays Music: Auditory–motor Interactions in Music Perception and Production'. *Nature Reviews Neuroscience* 8, 547–58.

Zbikowski, L. (2008) 'Metaphor and Music' in R. W. Gibbs, Jr (ed.) *The Cambridge Handbook of Metaphor and Thought*. Cambridge: Cambridge University Press, 502–24.

— (2009) 'Music, Language, and Multimodal Metaphor' in C. Forceville and E. Urios-Aparisi (eds) *Multimodal Metaphor*. Berlin: Mouton de Gruyter, 359–81.

Index

accompaniment (musical), 23, 72, 103
action effect, 66–9, 73, 76, 78, 81
action research, 13–16, 18, 109, 118–22
Agawu, Kofi, 26
Aiello, Rita, 47–8, 59
Anderson, Gary, 14
attunement, 93, 98–101, 103, 105, 107, 110–11, 115, 124

backward conditioning *see* ideomotor principle
Barber, Samuel, 17, 32, 42–3, 53, 70–72, 102–6
Barthes, Roland, 11
Barry, Nancy, 77
bass trombone *see* trombone
Belbin, Meredith, 31, 34
Berliner, Paul, 98
Birmingham Conservatoire, xiii, xviii, 16–17, 31, 42, 111, 120
body language, 20, 26, 37–9, 99
Boult Quartet, the, xiii, 17–18, 20, 31–2, 42–3, 49–50, 53, 55, 70, 72, 80, 92, 97, 102, 106
Bowie, Andrew, 125
Burns, James, 6, 33
Brydon-Miller, Mary, 13, 16, 120–21

Carmina Quartet, 29
Centre for Musical Performance as Creative Practice, 119
Clarke, Eric, 23–5, 40
Colman, Andrew, 2, 29
comedy, 86
communication
    between ensemble members, 19–20, 24, 36, 42–3, 59, 61, 66, 95, 98, 105–7, 114
    between performer and audience, 19, 24–6, 36, 42

intention and, 45, 63, 94, 97, 101, 106
modes, 3–4, 6–7, 19–20, 39, 42, 59, 73
musical, 19
nonverbal, 3, 6–7, 19–20, 38–42
paradigms of, 6–7, 20, 22–8, 41–5, 47, 60–61, 83, 87, 97–8, 100, 102, 109, 115–16, 124
verbal, 3–4, 6, 19–20, 27, 51, 91–2
visual, 7, 40, 42
communitas, 21, 101, 116, 124
conducting, 10, 24, 35, 38, 58–9, 106–7
Conflict Paradox, 29–30
Conlon, Donald, 29–30
Cook, Nicholas, 25
Cross, Ian, 26
cue, 20, 25, 35–40, 105–7, 124

Dahl, Sofia, 69–70, 74
Davidson, Jane, 8, 23–8, 35–8, 40, 66, 79
decoding, 7, 26, 42, 44
Dewey, John, 49, 86–7, 96
Dogantan-Dack, Mine, 73
double- and triple-loop learning, 118

Ekman, Paul, 25, 115
Elsdon, Peter, 27–8
Elsner, Birgit, 66–7
embodiment, 51, 54, 63, 73, 75, 80–81, 83–7, 94–5, 99–101, 106–9, 112, 116, 122, 125
emic/etic *see* insider/outsider dichotomy
emotion, 21–2, 25–8, 47
encoding, 7, 42, 44, 83, 98, 100–102
experiment (method), 8–9, 11, 89, 121
eye contact *see* visual contact

feedback loop, 28, 77–8, 80, 85
Fish, Stanley, 45, 92
flamenco, 34, 36
flow, 77, 79, 101

foot tapping, 37
Friesen, Wallace, 25, 115
Frykholm, Gunilla, 68–9, 73, 86, 88–90,
    93–4, 96, 116

Garnett, Liz, 10, 37
gesture
    adaptive, 25
    categorization/taxonomy, 3, 18, 23, 27,
        38, 45, 52, 60, 95, 124
    communicative, 7, 9, 23, 28, 42, 44–5,
        60, 106–7, 124
    conducting, 24, 58–9, 106
    definition, 24, 98, 124
        and coordination, 38, 121, 123
        and expression/emotion, 24–5, 27
    illustrative/emblematic, 25
    interpretation of, 24–7, 35–6, 54, 87,
        106, 124
    preparatory, 73
    regulatory, 25
    repertoire, 24, 35
    sound-accompanying, 6, 23, 106
    sound-facilitating, 6, 23
    sound-producing, 6, 23, 40–41, 70–71,
        78–9, 85, 99, 106
    speech, in 6, 24, 27
    study of, 12, 23, 28, 115–16, 120
Gilboa, Avi, 34, 42
Ginsborg, Jane, 23, 27, 37, 106
Godøy, Rolf, 24, 50, 54, 85–7, 94
Goodman, Elaine *see* King, Elaine
graphic notation, 57, 59
Gritten, Anthony, 23
group roles, 7, 33–4, 61, 72, 91–2, 111,
    116–17
Guarneri String Quartet, 29, 37, 73, 91,
    97–9

Hallam, Susan, 77
Halmrast, Tor, 52, 77–8
Hatten, Robert, 98
Hellaby, Julian, 65
Heron, John, 11
Herr, Kathryn, 14
Histoire du Soldat, 95
Hoffmann, Joachim, 67
Hommel, Bernhard, 66–7

Huang, Hilary, 15

ideomotor principle, 67–9, 80
improvisation, 9, 70, 84, 95–6, 99, 103,
    110–13
individual practice, 75, 77–80, 99
inference, 9, 58, 61, 86–90, 92–7, 99–103,
    105–7, 111, 114, 116, 123–4
insider/outsider dichotomy, 12, 14
intention
    and action, 21, 42, 45–6, 65–7, 75, 79,
        83, 92, 99, 101
    attributed/perceived, 7, 9, 46, 81, 84,
        87–8, 90, 92–3, 95, 97, 106–7, 114,
        124
    and communication, 45, 101, 106
    and ethics, 92
    hierarchy of, 64, 117
    musical/performative, 5, 9, 38,
        43–4, 54, 63, 65–6, 69–70, 72–3,
        75–7, 79, 81, 83–4, 88, 90–93, 95,
        99–103, 105, 107, 111–14, 123–4
    operative, 45–6
    personal, 7, 45, 64–7, 84, 87–8, 90;
    shared, 13, 88, 90–92, 100, 107,
        111–12, 115–17, 124
inter-reaction, 100–103, 105–7, 109–14,
    116–17, 123–5
interpretation, 8, 29–30, 32, 35, 38, 44–5,
    47–8, 51–4, 57–8, 63, 66, 74–5, 83,
    85, 87–8, 96–101, 103–5, 110–13,
    116–17, 122–4
interpretative coordination, 8, 19, 32,
    36, 45, 91, 97, 100, 103–5, 107,
    111–12, 115–16, 124
interview, 7, 9–12, 15–17, 29, 34, 103

Jäncke, Lutz, 47, 94
jazz, 2, 17, 27, 31–2, 58, 95, 99
Jensenius, Alexander, 6, 23–4, 28, 45, 70
Jerde, Thomas, 68
Johnson, Mark, 7, 49, 51–3, 55, 61, 75,
    87, 123

Keller, Peter, 78–9
Kemmis, Stephen, 13, 122
kinematic specification of dynamics,
    88–90, 95–6

King, Elaine, 8, 23, 27, 31, 34–8, 99
Kivy, Peter, 27, 44, 63, 81, 86
knowing-in-action, 72
knowledge
    ecological, 68, 85–7
    modes, 11–12, 14–18, 30, 41–2, 45,
        47, 57, 60–61, 63, 68–69, 72–7,
        80–81, 83–4, 88, 94, 100, 108–9,
        112, 117–25
    procedural, xviii, 4, 11, 17–18, 41, 73,
        75, 85, 121
    propositional, xviii, 4, 11, 17–18, 39,
        41, 45, 47, 60, 68, 72, 75–7, 80, 84,
        94–5, 108, 112, 122
Koch, Iring, 78–9
Kühl, Ole, 27

Lakoff, George, 7, 49, 51–3, 55, 61, 75,
    87, 123
leadership, 6–7, 20, 29–39, 41, 45, 60–61,
    103, 113, 116–17, 124
    alternating, 33–4, 38, 61, 91–2, 101,
        116–17
    balance of, 32–5, 91–2, 101
    charismatic, 31
    contextual, 31
    developmental contexts, 30–33, 41,
        117, 124
    example, by 38–9, 41, 44, 105, 107, 115
    experiential, 31
    gesture, through 6, 30, 35–8
    musical, 6, 29, 32, 104–5
    study of, 116–17
    transformational, 33–4, 39
    transactional, 33–4, 38–9
    verbal, 6, 33–5
Leman, Marc, 12, 24, 69, 79

MacDonald, Raymond, 95
McNeill, David, 24, 27, 115–16
Manduell, Mariana, 34, 36
mental imagery, 50, 52, 54, 57, 76, 78
Merleau-Ponty, Maurice, 45
metaphor, 7, 26, 48–59, 61, 74–8, 83, 85,
    95, 124–5
Meyer, Leonard, 47
mistake, 83, 93
motion capture, 10–11

multimodality, 44, 53–5, 58–9, 61, 77, 85,
    88, 95, 102, 107, 123
Murnighan, Keith, 29–30
music as language, 26–7
musical analysis, 7, 71–2, 84, 122–3
musical imagination, 52, 54–5, 76
musical information, 3–4, 19, 27–8, 37–8,
    40–41, 47–8, 58–61, 87–90, 94–6,
    98–100, 107, 124
musicality, 113–15
musicianship *see* musicality

Norton, Herter, 91, 113–14
notation, 29, 54, 57–9, 74–5

observation
    action research, within 13, 15–17, 122
    aural, 40, 96, 98, 100
    informed, 12, 95
    method, 6–7, 9–10, 12, 15–17, 29, 37,
        42–4, 111, 113, 122
opera, 25

participatory action research, 14–16, 122
pedagogy, 3, 11, 31–2, 39–40, 63, 65, 71,
    73–7, 81, 117–18
performance (participatory), 21–2, 101, 114
performance (presentational), 21–2, 65,
    77, 114
performance art, 26, 74
placeholder, 52, 54–5
popular music, 26–7
practitioner literature, 7, 9–12, 14, 98
preadjustment, 73, 90
propositional analysis, 47, 72, 75–7, 84–5,
    120, 123
propositional research *see* propositional
    analysis
pushing/pulling information, 42, 95, 120, 124

redundancy, 35
reflective journal, 16, 18
reflective practice, 13–19, 61, 79, 109,
    117–24
rehearsal language, 48–59, 76
Runeson, Sverker, 68–9, 73, 86, 88–90,
    93–4, 96, 116
Ryle, Gilbert, 11, 69

sameness *see* communitas
Sawyer, Keith, 99
Schön, Donald, 14, 18, 57, 72, 76, 118
Schneider, Albrecht, 26
score indications, 74
Seddon, Frederick, 6, 19–20, 39
Sloboda, John, 39
solo performance, 3, 5, 20, 23–4, 26–8, 35,
     39, 61, 75, 77, 81, 113, 115
string quartet, 20, 29, 32, 34, 38–9, 42–3,
     49, 53, 70–72, 98, 102–6
String Quartet No. 1, Op. 11: see Barber,
     Samuel
Supergroup, The xiii, 17–18, 20, 31, 70,
     111–12
survey *see* interview

Tal-Shmotkin, Malka, 34, 42
team cognition, 31
temporal synchronization, 2, 8, 36
timbre, 36, 49–50, 52, 54–5, 69, 74–5, 78
Tokyo String Quartet, 19
Tomasello, Michael, 64, 66, 90–91, 97, 117
Tovstiga, George, 29, 39–40, 98
trombone, 1, 17, 71, 78, 85–6, 94–5, 111,
     116–17, 119

Turino, Thomas, 21–2, 65, 101, 114–16

unconsciousness, 66, 75, 84, 93, 103, 112,
     117, 123
unintentionality, 44–5, 61, 64, 70, 93, 98, 101
University of Alaska, 17
University of Michigan, xvii, 17, 94

verbal discussion, 3–4, 51–2, 55–8
Vines, Bradley, 87
visual contact, 20, 37–9, 107
voice (instrument), 3, 77

Waltz of the Tearing Tears, 70, 111
Wanderley, Marcelo, 87
Western classical tradition, 1–2, 19–20,
     25–6, 29, 32, 37, 44, 57–8, 91
Wiesendanger, Mario, 10
Williamon, Aaron, 8, 37–8, 40
Wilson, Graeme, 95
Wing, Alan, 34, 36

Young, Vivienne, 2, 29